Folens
Words at Work ✓

Word-level and Sentence-level Work for Excellence in Spelling and Grammar

JO PHENIX

Hello! I am Buzzy Bee.
Welcome to
Words at Work ✓,
a book of activities and games
to help you to become a
better writer.

First published in the United Kingdom in 1999 by

Folens Publishers
Albert House
Apex Business Centre
Boscombe Road
Dunstable
Bedfordshire
LU5 4RL

Editors: Laura Dargie and Jennifer Steele   Layout artist: James Brown
Illustrations: Sarah Hedley (Graham-Cameron Illustration)
           Mike Lacey (Simon Girling & Associates)
           Liz Sawyer (Simon Girling & Associates)
           Sue Woollatt (Graham-Cameron Illustration)
Cover artist: Sue Woollatt   Page design: Turners Creative
Cover design: Martin Cross

British Library Cataloguing in Publication Data.
A catalogue record for this book is available from the British Library.
Printed in Hong Kong through World Print.

ISBN 1 86202 621-1
UK edition © Folens 1999.

Words at Work ✔

Contents

Building Words

Working With Words

Working With Sentences

Revision

Watch for the T

Say each of these words out loud, and listen to the sound at the end of each word:

- *porch* *catch*
- *bench* *pitch.*

Each word has the same sound at the end. You will see that there are two ways to spell this sound: **ch tch**.

A Find the words in the teapot that have a **short vowel** immediately before the **ch**. List them according to their short-vowel sound.

Copy and Complete				
a (like hat)	e (like elf)	i (like pin)	o (like doll)	u (like cup)

teach

catch fetch clutch

pitch perch search merchant

bench birch

hatch crotchety

Dutch

porch botch peach

speech sketch pinch ditch

launch hitch

patch bunch

ketchup

hopscotch

arch

- All your short-vowel words have **tch**. When you hear a short-vowel sound right before the **ch** sound, use **tch**.

B Now sort the other words. Look at the letters that come before the **ch** sound.

Copy and Complete		
r before the ch	n before the ch	Long-vowel sound before the ch

Remember The sound **ch** is spelled **tch** when it has a *short vowel* before it.

The Search for the Missing D

Say each of these words out loud, and listen to the sounds at the end of each word:

- *badger*   *page*
- *fudge*   *huge.*

Each word has the same sound. You will see that there are two ways to spell this sound: **ge**   **dge**.

- Words which have **dge** letter pattern have a short-vowel sound, for example **hedge**

- Words which have **ge** letter pattern have a long-vowel sound, for example **huge**.

A   From this wordsearch, choose the words that have a **short-vowel** sound before the **g** sound. List them according to their vowel sounds. The words run across and down. If you need to circle the words as you find them, carefully copy the wordsearch first.

Copy and Complete				
Short a	Short e	Short i	Short o	Short u
badge	hedge	ridge	dodge	fudge

w	b	r	f	l	e	d	g	e	e	l	w	s
c	a	g	e	x	h	i	n	g	e	d	j	t
b	d	h	e	d	g	e	t	d	b	o	i	r
r	g	e	o	r	g	e	o	u	u	d	s	a
i	e	u	m	f	b	n	l	n	d	g	i	n
d	v	r	a	u	u	u	o	n	g	e	e	g
g	l	g	d	d	l	d	d	m	e	r	g	e
e	a	e	g	g	g	g	g	v	t	s	e	r
e	d	g	e	e	e	e	e	r	i	d	g	e

B   Now sort the other words with **g** sounds.

Copy and Complete			
l before the g	r before the g	n before the g	Long-vowel sound before the g

C   How many other words can you add to each list?

Remember If you want to know when to use **dge**, listen for the *short-vowel* sound.

5

Up the Creek ... !

We often confuse the word endings **le** and **el** as they sound the same. Most words which have this sound end in **le**. It is a good idea to record all those that end in **el**. For example:

● *twinkle* but *quarrel*.

You should also remember to double the **l** when you add a **suffix** beginning with a **vowel** to words ending in **el,** like this:

● *quarrelling quarrelled.*

A Read the following story. How many **el/le** spelling mistakes can you find? There are 12. Write them down correctly.

Up The Creek ... !

Rachle's Uncel Bill was very singel-minded. He would travle to any destination if it meant an adventure. He had trundelled through the jungles of the rainforest, travelled to the middel of the Sahara desert, tunnled through potholes, wobbled on a tightrope across Niagara Falls and struggelled to reach the top of Mount Everest.

Now Rachel discovered that he was about to take another gambel and channle his way up a dangerous creek without a paddel.

''Simpel!'' shouted Uncle Bill as Rachel waved him goodbye ...

B Write a final paragraph for the story. Include the following words if you can:

muddle	ankle	tumbled	grumbled
	squirrel	shovelled	towel

Remember It is easy to confuse words that end in **le** and **el**.

Word Pyramids

A Copy the words below and add a letter in each row to make new words. Each row must repeat the letters of the word above to build rhyming patterns.

For example:

1. rain
<u>t</u>rain
<u>st</u>rain

2. ate
_ate
_ _ate

3. aid
_aid
_ _aid

4. see
see_
s_ee_

5. sigh
sigh_
s_igh_

6. oil
_oil
_ _oil

7. hoping
hop_ing
_hop_ing

8. row
_row
row

9. cat
c_at
c_a_t

10. one
_one
_ _one

11. ice
_ice
_ _ice

12. ray
_ray
_ _ray

13. eat
_ eat
_ _eat

14. too
too_
too

15. too
too_
too_ _

16. tea
tea_
tea

17. eel
_eel
_ _eel

When were there only three letters in the alphabet?

Before U and I were born!

Remember Building *rhyming patterns* will help you to spell correctly.

Rhyme Time

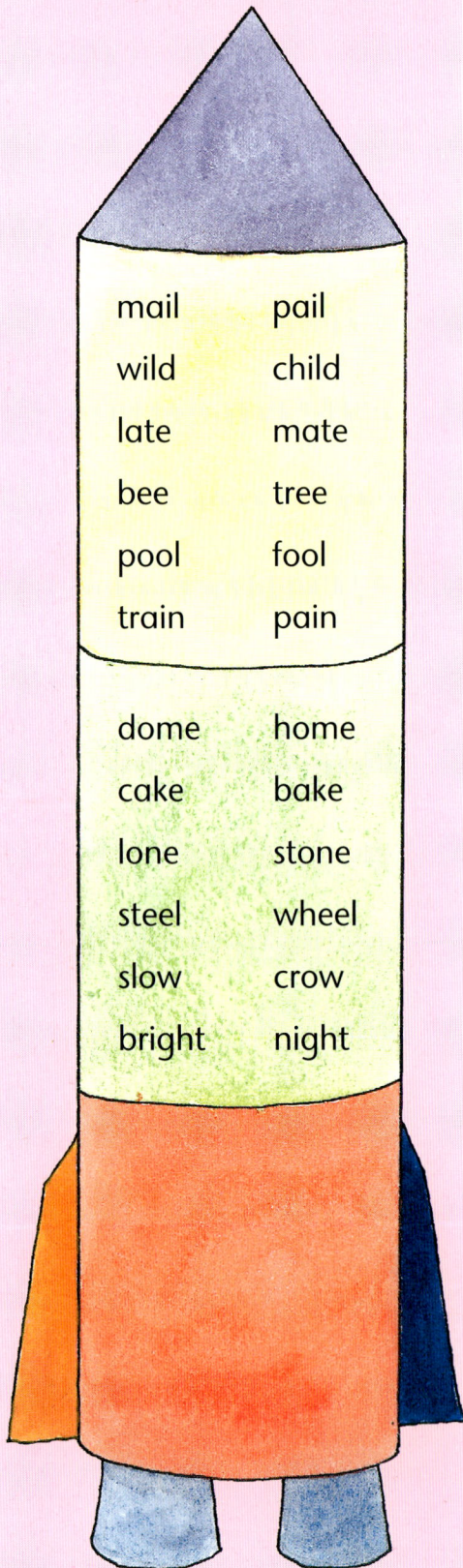

A Solve each riddle with a pair of rhyming words. You will find the words hidden in the space rocket. Hɪɴᴛ: Each pair of words will have the same **long-vowel** spelling pattern.

mail	pail
wild	child
late	mate
bee	tree
pool	fool
train	pain
dome	home
cake	bake
lone	stone
steel	wheel
slow	crow
bright	night

Copy and Complete

1. A friend who does not arrive on time.　　　　late mate

1. A friend who does not arrive on time.

2. Someone who misbehaves when swimming.

3. A single rock.

4. A house shaped like half a ball.

5. A black bird which takes a long time to arrive.

6. A bucket full of letters.

7. An oak or birch containing a hive.

8. Travel sickness on rails.

9. Cooking special food for a birthday party.

10. A metal part of your bicycle.

11. Full moon.

12. A badly behaved infant.

Remember Learning words in *families* will help to improve your spelling.

Weather Compounds

A How many **compound words** can you build using each of these weather words?

Copy and Complete		
a. snow	**b.** rain	**c.** ice
snowstorm		
d. sun	**e.** thunder	**f.** wind

B Write a weather report for today. How many of your weather compounds can you use?

Remember A *compound word* is made up of two smaller words.

Animal Compounds

A Write a **compound word** using each animal's name.

1. horse

2. dragon

3. dog

4. cat

5. fly

6. fish

7. frog

8. snake

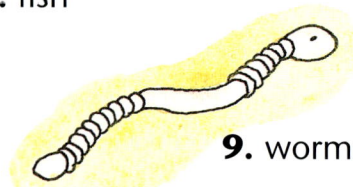

9. worm

B List any other compound words you can think of which use an animal's name.

Remember A *compound word* is made up of two smaller words.

Prefix Opposites

A **prefix** is a group of letters added at the beginning of a word. The same prefix can often be used with many different words.

Always add a prefix to the whole word. Do not leave out any letters.

A Find words in the wordsearch to complete the words started by the prefixes below. When you add the prefix to each word, it will make its **opposite**. The words go across and down. If you need to circle the words as you find them, carefully copy the wordsearch first.

Prefixes						
ir	**un**	**im**	**de**	**in**	**mis**	**il**

r	e	s	p	o	n	s	i	b	l	e	b
e	q	u	a	l	d	o	c	r	e	v	r
p	o	s	s	i	b	l	e	e	g	e	e
l	c	s	p	e	l	l	i	a	a	n	a
a	c	c	u	r	a	t	e	t	l	i	k
c	u	c	l	i	m	b	a	b	l	e	a
e	p	u	m	o	v	a	b	l	e	r	b
a	i	t	r	e	g	u	l	a	r	a	l
b	e	a	s	y	c	l	e	a	n	b	e
l	d	a	c	c	e	s	s	i	b	l	e
e	b	e	l	i	e	v	a	b	l	e	r
r	e	l	e	v	a	n	t	b	e	b	l

What might you call a sick bird?

An ill eagle!

Remember Always add a *prefix* to the whole word.

Excellent Prefixes

A Use the **prefix ex** and a word chunk from the cat to form words to complete these sentences.

Copy and Complete

1. All the months have 30 or 31 days <u>except</u> February.

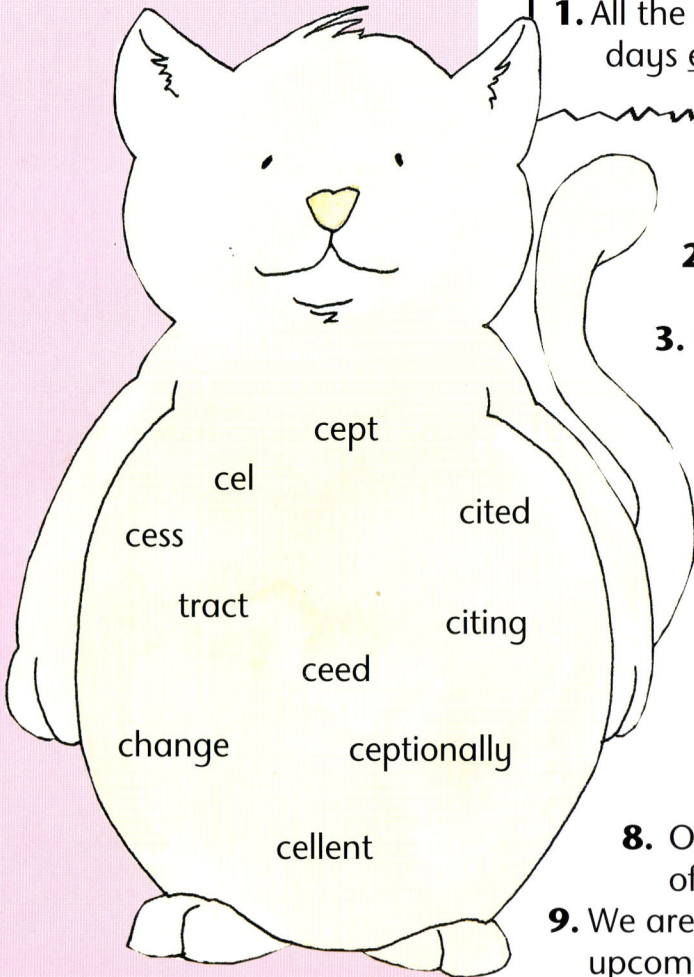

---

1. All the months have 30 or 31 days _____ February.

2. If the coat doesn't fit your dog, bring it back and I will _____ it.

3. It was the closest and most _____ game of the season.

4. We always remind Dad not to _____ the speed limit.

5. This past winter was an _____ cold one in our area.

6. Swimming is an _____ form of exercise.

7. I am planning to read aloud an _____ from my story at the concert.

8. Our cat is on a diet to get rid of her _____ fat.

9. We are all _____ about the upcoming trip.

10. Catherine was so talented she seemed to _____ at everything.

The cat word chunks:
cept, cel, cess, cited, tract, citing, ceed, change, ceptionally, cellent

B How many other words can you write that have the prefix **ex** followed by a **soft c**? (A soft **c** sounds like **s**.)

Remember Don't forget the **c** when you add the *prefix* **ex** to word chunks beginning with **c**.

Prefix Maths

A Use the meanings of the **prefixes** on this page to help you to solve the maths questions. Write out your answers and add up the totals.

1.

Add:

a. Wheels on a unicycle.

b. Years in a century.

c. Events in a decathlon.

What is your total?

2.

Add:

a. Performers in a duet.

b. Quarters in a whole.

c. Years in a decade.

What is your total?

3.

a. Quadruple the number of sides on a pentagon.

b. Triple the legs of a quadruped.

c. A quarter of the tentacles of an octopus.

d. The sides on ten pentagons.

e. Subtract the sides on a hexagon from an octagon.

What is your total?

Remember Many words in maths have *prefixes*. Learning their meanings will help your maths and spelling.

Magnified Prefixes

The **prefixes micro**, **mini**, **maxi** and **mega** all tell you about the size of what they are attached to.

A **megalith** is a big rock.

Have you read the new book 'Making the Most of Your Life' by Maxie Mumm?

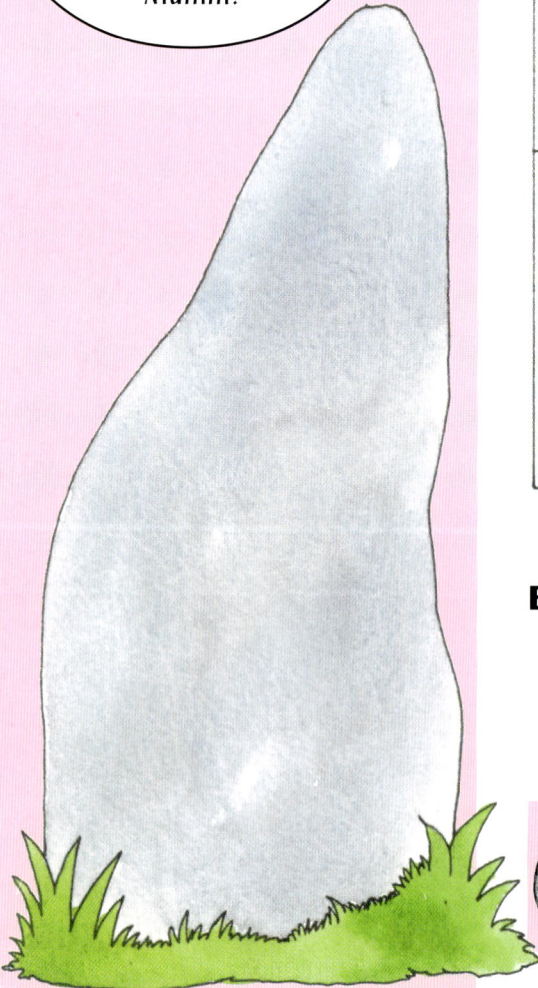

A Build words using the prefixes **mini**, **micro** and **mega** to write labels for these pictures.

1.
2.
3.
4.
5.
6.

B Which two prefixes mean large? Which two prefixes mean small? What other words do you know that use these prefixes?

Remember Some *prefixes* will tell you the size of something.

14

Shared Roots

Finding **roots** and **prefixes** can help you to understand what words mean. It can also help you to spell them correctly.

A Use the meaning of these roots to write definitions for the highlighted words or answer the questions. Then add another word using the same root. Use a dictionary if you need to.

1. Man means by hand.
What does it mean to do a job **manually**?

2. Trans means across.
Name one country to which you could make a **transatlantic** phone call.

3. Uni means one. **Form** means shape.
What does it mean if you describe some things as **uniform**?

4. Vac means empty.
How would you **vacate** a room?
What does it mean to say that space is a **vacuum**?

5. Struct means to build. **Con** means together.
What does **construction** mean?
What does **destruction** mean?

6. Mand means to order.
What would you give to order someone to do something?

7. Mech means machine.
What would you call a person who repairs machines?

Remember Knowing the meaning of *roots* and *prefixes* can help you to spell correctly.

Get to the Root

cap = head

ped = foot

rupt = break

sign = mark

spec = see

tract = pull

vis = see

A Some **roots** come from other languages. The roots on this page all come from **Latin**. Write out the sentences below and complete them using a root from the boxes opposite.

1. The head person of a team may be called a _____ .

2. When you ride a bicycle, you put each foot on a _____ .
   Someone on foot in the street is called a _____ .

3. When lava pours from a volcano, it is called an _____ .
   When you break into someone's conversation you are _____ .

4. Your personal mark at the bottom of a letter is your _____ .

5. You can wear a pair of _____ to help you see better.
   You can _____ something closely to see if it is all right.

6. A vehicle that pulls other machinery is a _____ .
   When you take one number away from another you _____ .

7. You can see entertainment in your home on a _____ .
   When you go to see a friend or relative you _____ them.

Remember Some Latin *root words* are not complete words. Their meanings will help your spelling.

Latin Labels

A Write down what each of these pictures represents using a word containing one or more of these Latin **roots**:

sub = under **extra** = outside **mar** = sea
dent = tooth **aqua** = water **fac** = make
spec = see **mob** = move **multi** = many
ped = foot **rupt** = break **sign** = mark
sta = stand **tract** = pull **vis** = see
auto = by itself

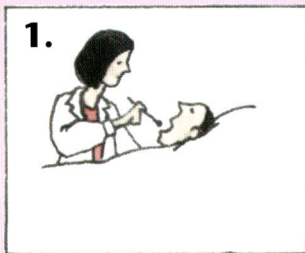

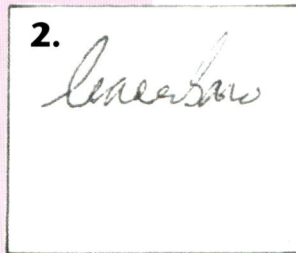

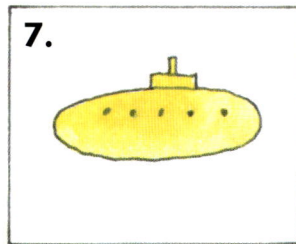

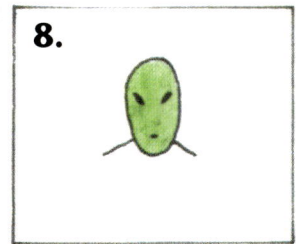

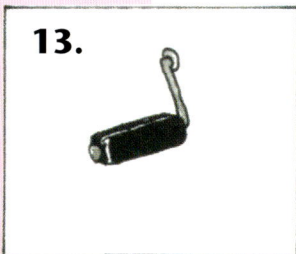

1.	2.	3.	4.
5.	6.	7.	8.
9.	10.	11.	12.
	13.	14.	

Remember Knowing the meaning of words will help you spell to them.

Grow Some Roots

Words are made up of beats of sound called **syllables**. For instance, the word *box* has just one syllable, and the word *surprise* has two syllables – **sur-prise**. The word *elephant* has three syllables – **el-e-phant**.

A How many words can you build using each of these Greek **roots**?

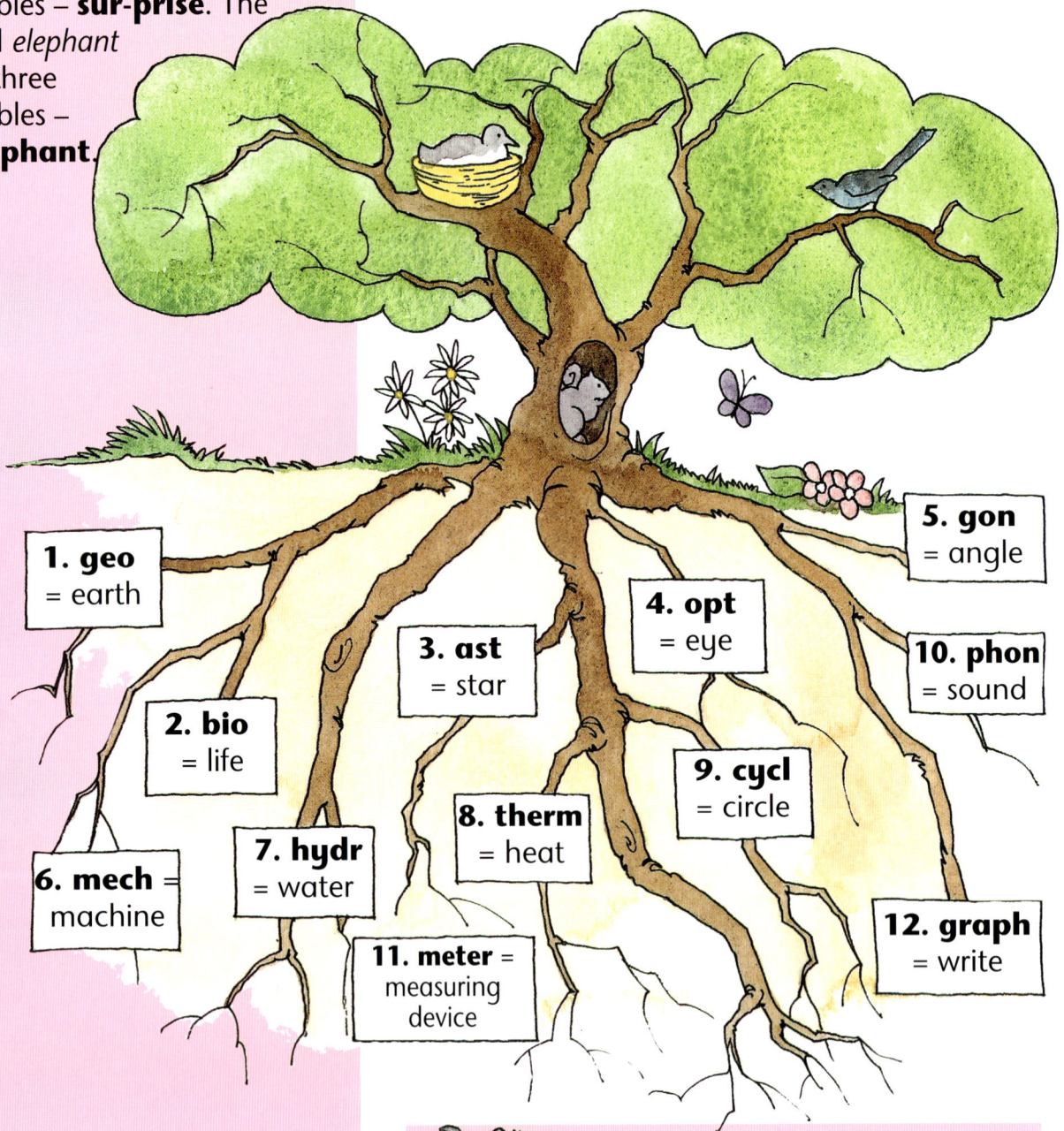

1. geo = earth

2. bio = life

3. ast = star

4. opt = eye

5. gon = angle

6. mech = machine

7. hydr = water

8. therm = heat

9. cycl = circle

10. phon = sound

11. meter = measuring device

12. graph = write

Remember Some Greek *roots* are not complete words. Learn their meanings. They will help your spelling.

Adding Endings

Prefixes are parts of words that attach to the beginnings of roots.

Suffixes are parts of words that attach to the ends of roots. For example:

- prefix + root + suffix
  re + *build* + *ing*
  rebuilding.

A There are three special patterns to remember when you add endings beginning with vowels.

1. When the final **syllable** has a **short vowel**, you double the last letter:
   - *scrub scrubbing*.
2. When the last sound of the word is **y** by itself, you change the **y** to **i**:
   - *baby babies*.
3. When the word has a **silent e** at the end, you drop the **e**:
   - *like liking*.

- For all other words, just add the ending:
  - *catch catching*.

- Add as many of the endings below as you can to each of the words on the jigsaw pieces.

ed	ing	able	en
al	ery	er	est

For example:
like   liked   liking   likable   liken.

Remember The patterns for *suffixes* ending in vowels are:
- if the final *syllable* has a *short vowel*, double the last letter
- if the last sound of the word is **y** by itself, change the **y** to **i**
- if the word has a silent **e** at the end, drop the **e**.

wide
care
desire
short
use
delay
ride
sharp
enjoy
bake
try
fine
ripe
like

Suffix Maths

A Copy the 'suffix sums' below and make new words by completing them. Think about all the **patterns** you have learned for adding endings to words. Be careful, some are addition and some are minus!

Copy and complete

Level 1
a. use + ful = ?
b. wise + ly = ?
c. slow + ly = ?
d. catch + ing = ?
e. boy + ish = ?
f. kind + est = ?

Level 2
a. drop + ed = ?   **h.** fix + ed = ?
b. hum + ing = ?   **i.** try + ed = ?
c. hop + ing = ?   **j.** steady + est = ?
d. hope + ing = ?   **k.** silly + ness = ?
e. drive + er = ?   **l.** plenty + ful = ?
f. mix + er = ?   **m.** lucky + ly = ?
g. fax + ing = ?

Level 3
a. running – ing = ?
b. safer – er + ty = ?
c. hurried – ed = ?
d. festival – al = ?
e. simply – ly = ?
f. nastiness – nasty + hasty = ?
g. easily – ly = ?
h. fun + y + er = ?
i. hitter – er = ?

Remember There are *patterns* for adding endings to words.

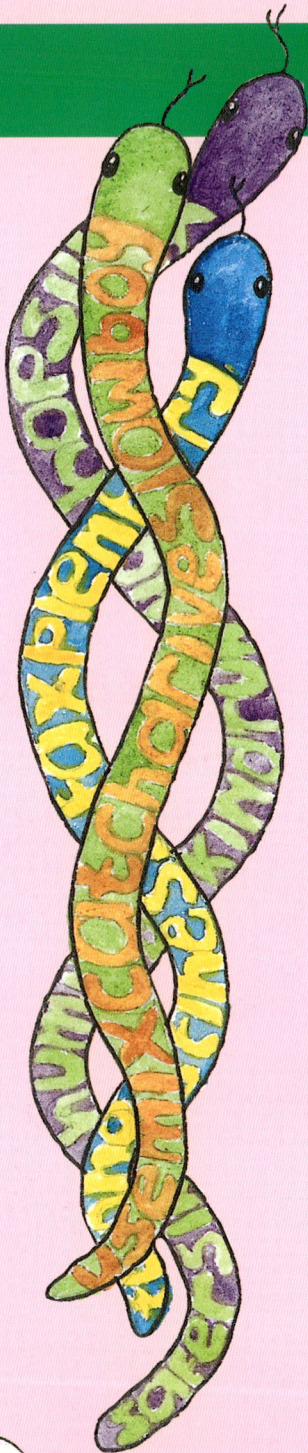

What snakes are good at arithmetic?

Adders.

My Holiday

The first day of my holiday we went to see a magician. The next day we rented an action film about aliens on a mission to set up space stations. After that we went camping for a week. It was lots of fun, with the exception of when our dalmatian tipped the canoe over and all our possessions went floating down the river.

We had to collect them all and dry them out!

Just before I came back to school, my family and I went to an amazing concert. The best musician was in the percussion section. He could juggle the drumsticks while he played! That really made an impression on my sister and me.

A The writer has used many words that end with a **suffix** that sounds like 'shun'. Find each word and write it in the appropriate list. There are four ways to spell this sound in a suffix.

Copy and Complete			
cian	**ssion**	**tian**	**tion**

B Can you add one or two of your own words to each list?

C Write out these clues and their answers:
   a. A birthday is a special _____ .
   b. $9 \div 3 = 3$ is _____ .
   c. Decide, and make a _____ .

Remember All these *suffixes* sound like 'shun': **cian, tian, tion, ssion**.

What Can You Do?

A You can recognise words that end in **or** by linking them with 'shun' words. Use a word ending in **or** to identify each of these occupations:

Copy and Complete

1. If you help someone get an education, you are an _____ .

1. If you help someone get an education, you are an _____ .
2. If you create inventions, you are an _____ .
3. If you conduct investigations, you are an _____ .
4. If your job is supervision, you are a _____ .
5. If you tell people which direction to go in, you are a _____ .
6. If you are in charge of distribution, you are a _____ .
7. If you love aviation, you may be an _____ .
8. If you are part of the action on stage, you are an _____ .
9. If you have a collection, you are a _____ .
10. If you make an inspection, you are an _____ .
11. If you make predictions, you are a _____ .
12. If you work in administration, you are an _____ .

B List any other occupations you know which end in **or**.

Remember Many words ending in **or** are linked to words ending in the 'shun' sound.

Syllable Poems

A Here is a poem about a football game. As you read it, count the **syllables** in each line. How many syllables are there in each sentence?

Saturday
Football day.
Warm up first,
Kick the ball,
Striker strikes,
Scores a goal,
Jumps around,
Wins the game!

B Write more poems with three syllables per line. Start with 'Summer's Here'. Then choose three more titles of your own.

C You might like to try writing two-syllable or four-syllable poems.

Remember Splitting a word into *syllables* will help you to remember the spelling.

Three, Four or Five?

Longer words have more **syllables** and are often harder to spell, but you can use the syllables to help you.

Say this word. It can be a tongue-twister!

● *perpendicular*

If we split it into its parts it is easier to say:

● **per-pen-dic-ul-ar**.

We can also remember the spelling more easily.

A First group the words below under the headings shown in the 'Copy and Complete' chart, then split them into syllables. Check the meanings in a dictionary of those words you do not know.

Copy and Complete		
Mathematics	Geography	History
calculation		
cal-cu-la-tion		

calculation	Victorian	hexagon
artefact	temperature	agriculture
symmetry	geographical	geometrical
seasonal	chronological	locality
probability	civilisation	parliament

B Find ten smaller words in the longer ones. For example, you can find the words *hex*, *axe*, *age* and *gone* in *hexagon*.

After a couple of days, check how many of these words you can spell.

Remember Splitting words into their *syllables* and knowing their meanings will help you to remember the spelling.

More Spelling Tips

Sometimes **syllables** can be **prefixes** or **suffixes**. If you learn to spell these, you will find it easier to spell the whole word.

A How many words can you make? Match the prefixes in column **a** to the rest of the word in column **b** and write the whole word down. Some will match more than one. For example, **aero** will join with the suffixes **space** and **plane**.

a	b
aero	ane
audi	pod
bi	space
con	gen
cred	way
hydro	plane
oct	claim
sub	ceps
tri	it
ex	o
in	tain

● Check in a dictionary any words that you do not know.

B Now make words by adding prefixes to these suffixes:

hood	graph	port	scope	ware

Why are these suffixes also roots?

Remember Learning *prefixes* and *suffixes* can help you with your spelling.

Orang-Utan's Lucky Day

You can help yourself to remember awkward words by using **mnemonics** (pronounced **nem-on-ic**).

For example:

● **h**orses **a**nd **p**retty **p**onies **y**awn

is a mnemonic for *happy*.

Usually it is a particular part of a word that we need to focus on, such as:

● **o**rang-**u**tan's **l**ucky **d**ay.

This could help you to remember:

● c**ould** w**ould** sh**ould.**

A Work out these mnemonics and write down the words:

1. golden onions every spring
2. count on me I never gossip
3. the orang-utan's green home
4. serve up raspberry pie regularly in silver eggcups

B Make up mnemonics for the parts of these words written in bold:

a. lib**rar**y	**b.** Wed**nes**day	**c.** an**gel**
d. Feb**ru**ary	**e.** circ**uit**	**f.** autu**mn**

C Think of five words you often spell wrongly. Make up a mnemonic for the part of the word that you get wrong. Keep them in a spelling bank.

Do orang-utans guzzle honey? (dough)

GUZZLE'S HONEY, NATURE'S FINEST

Remember *Mnemonics* can help you to recall awkward spellings.

26

Whither and Thither

There are many English words we no longer use and others we use in different ways because language changes over time. This is to do with new inventions, new ideas and changes in manners and fashion.

However, it is surprisingly easy to work out what some of these words mean, even words that were used hundreds of years ago.

Some words that we use today had **st** and **th** endings attached to them:

- *wouldst* means *would*
- *cometh* means *come*.

A   Try to work out what these words mean:

endeth	thou	oft
loveth	tellen	writ
thereto	goeth	whither
yonder	thither	quoth

B   Read with a partner the following heated conversation. Try to work out what is happening. Write out the conversation in modern English.

''How now, good sir, how now?''

''Away you rogue! Call'st me thou 'good sir'? You viper vile!''

''What say'st thou? Viper is't? Have you your wits? Know you to whom you speak?''

''Aye, viper. You rascal, you imp! I will inflame your liver and make you rage!''

Remember Words and expressions change over time.

What's in a Name?

Many **proper names** of people have their origins in the distant past:

- *Peter* is a Christian name meaning *rock*.
- *Deepak* is a Hindu name meaning *light*.

Many English surnames originally related to a person's characteristics, where they lived or the job they did:

- *Short   Hill   Miller.*

Sometimes a name could be built up over time. For example:

- *Wilkinson.*

Wil refers to *William*, **kin** can mean *little* or *family*, therefore *Wilkinson* could mean either:

- son of little William, or
- a son of the William family.

Title	Meaning
Ap	son of (Welsh)
O'	of (Irish)
Mac	son of (Scottish)
Mc	son of (Irish)

A Using the information in the chart above and on the page, work out what these names could mean:

Robertson	David ap Evan	Macdonald
O'Brian	Dale O'Donnell	Fair
Bridges	Moore O'Neil	Tomkinson
Gray	Michaelson McGlade	Taylor
Long	Baker Redhead	

- Why do you think 'son of' rather than 'daughter of' is common?

B Find out the meaning of these names:

Penny	Jason	Peter	Leroy
Finn	Diana	Timothy	Maria
Jade	Pooja	Selena	

Remember *Proper names* can have meanings.

Place Names

Like people's names, **place names** also have meanings. Their meanings can tell us about the origins of a place. For example, **by** at the end of a name is very common. It is Viking and means a *farm* or *village*.

- *Eastby* would probably have been a *farm* or *village* in the *East*.

Places

Word	Meaning
borough, burgh, bury	fort
ford	river crossing
ham	small village
mere	lake
stead	homestead
aber	mouth of river
thwaite	clearing
thorp	farm
toft	plot of ground
wick	dairy
llan	church or parish
fawr	great
St Illtud	Welsh saint

A   Use the information in the chart above and on the page and also your own knowledge to work out what these names could mean:

Northwick	Oxford	Inverness
Burghill	Greatham	Littleham
Highbury	Eastoft	Fairlight Cove
Portsmouth	Aberystwyth	Woodthorpe
Mountain Ash	Llanilltud Fawr	East Mere
Southborough	Thwaite	
Greenstead Green		

B   The English version of Llanilltud Fawr is Llantwit Major. Work out the links between the two names.

Remember *Place names* have meanings.

Solomon Grundy, Born on Monday

Like proper names and place names, **days of the week** have hidden meanings. These meanings have their **origins** in history, sometimes from different cultures and languages.

A Draw up a table like this:

Copy and Complete		
	Meaning	Further Information
Sunday		
Monday		
Tuesday		
Wednesday		
Thursday		
Friday		
Saturday		

- **Meanings:**
  - Thor, god of thunder
  - Woden, chief god
  - Moon
  - Freya, goddess of fertility
  - Saturn
  - Sun
  - Tiw, god of war.

- Decide which meaning fits each day and write it in your table. Use an encyclopaedia to find out more about the origin of each day.

B Complete the rhymes below and try to find out how old they are.
1. Solomon Grundy,
   Born on Monday ...
2. Monday's child is fair of face,
   Tuesday's child is full of grace ...

C Write a modern rhyme of your own for the days of the week.

Remember The *days of the week* have historical *origins*.

The Calendar

The 12 months of the year have **Latin** names. They have their origins in the **Roman calendar**.

novem, ninth month in the Roman calendar.
Janus, god of gateways and beginnings. He had two faces looking forwards and backwards.
Julius Caesar, Roman leader and general.
septem, seventh month in the Roman calendar.
Aprilis, aperire – to open – when the buds open.
Februa, a feast of cleansing.
octo, eighth month in the Roman calendar.
Maia, goddess worshipped in the last month of spring, linked to the god Vulcan.
Juno, most important goddess, wife of Jupiter.
decem, tenth month of the Roman calendar.
Caesar Augustus, first Roman emperor.
Martius, Mars, god of war.

A   Draw up a table of months like this:

Copy and Complete		
Month	Latin name	Meaning
January	Janus	The beginning of the year.

● Decide which Latin name fits each month of the year and write it under the heading. Select information and add it to your table.

B   Guess the meaning of these words from the information you have. Then check them in a dictionary.

volcano	septet	octane
janitor	decimal	Martian

C   Work with a partner or a group. Design a calendar with suitable symbols for each month.

Remember The months of the year have their origins in the **Roman calendar**.

Every Dog Has Its Day

Proverbs are wise sayings. They usually have hidden messages about life, told in a clever and amusing way. Most have been around for a long time and have not changed. For example:

● We never miss the water till the well runs dry.

This means that we do not appreciate what we have until it has gone.

A Read this **proverb poem** with a partner and guess what the lines could mean. Check in a dictionary any words you do not know.

Every Dog Has Its Day

A wild goose never laid a tame egg,
Better half a loaf than no bread,
Cut your coat according to your cloth,
Too many cooks spoil the broth,
In for a penny, in for a pound,
Empty vessels make the most sound,
More haste less speed,
A friend in need is a friend indeed,
Once bitten, twice shy,
We never miss the water till the well runs dry,
Pride goes before a fall,
Robbing Peter to pay Paul,
Far from court, far from care,
None but the brave deserve the fair,
Where there's a will there's a way,
When the cat's away the mice will play,
And ...
Every dog has its day!

Mary Green

B Does your family have any sayings? Do you know any proverbs from other cultures? Write them down.

C Make up some proverbs of your own and ask your partner to guess what they mean.

Remember *Proverbs* are sayings which have hidden messages.

Park or Playground?

Sometimes we have to say whether or not we agree with something and why. In other words, we need to **argue our case**. Read the following:

> Pets should not be kept in quarantine when they return to Britain. They are often housed in poor conditions and become ill. The period of quarantine is too long for an animal.
>
> Pets can carry rabies and infect wildlife and we need to prevent this ...

The passage above is not clear. In the second paragraph, the writer seems to change views. Now read the passage again:

> **In my view**, pets should not be kept in quarantine when they return to Britain. They are often housed in poor conditions and become ill. **In addition**, the period of quarantine is too long for an animal.
>
> **However, while I agree** that pets can carry rabies and infect wildlife and we need to prevent this, there are other measures ...

The words in bold help us to present ideas without contradicting ourselves.

A Complete this task:

There is a disused plot of land in your local area which is going to be redeveloped as:
either
a garden with a pond, flowers, trees and benches where people can sit peacefully
or
an adventure playground for children aged three to twelve which would include a treehouse, large wooden climbing frame, a skateboarding area, a sandpit and so on.

● Decide what you think should happen to the land and write your argument. Use some of these words and phrases:

> similarly   whereas   however   furthermore
> by contrast   in addition   having said that
> while I agree/disagree   in my view

Remember We can use special words to help to present an **argument**.

33

Inventing Words

You can invent your own words! For example:

● *vaccaphobe.*

The **prefix vacca** means *cow* and the **suffix phobe** means *fear*. *Vaccaphobe* therefore means a fear of cows!

What could a nausling be?

A little ship.

A How many words can you invent using these prefixes and suffixes? Say what your new words mean.

Prefixes		Suffixes	
vacca	*cow*	**phobe**	*fear*
archi	*chief*	**able**	*fit*
bi	*double*	**acity**	*power*
counter	*against*	**ate**	*make*
demi	*half*	**craft**	*skill*
dom	*home*	**fare**	*way*
milli	*thousand*	**fast**	*firm*
naus	*ship*	**ling**	*little*
octo	*eight*	**nym**	*name*
ped	*foot*	**most**	*greatest*
poly	*many*	**red**	*rule*
psych	*mind*	**ric**	*region*
sac	*bag*	**urnal**	*belongs to*

B Now make a sentence using some of your words and explain what the sentence means. For example: The *demiling* fought the *milliacitous octonymed* beast. (The little half-creature fought the eight-named beast of a thousand powers.)

Remember *Prefixes* and *suffixes* have meanings.

What's Green and Makes You Itch?

You can make a **pun** if you play with words that sound similar but have different meanings.

A joke is often based on a pun or a **double meaning**:

- What's green and makes you itch? Spinach!

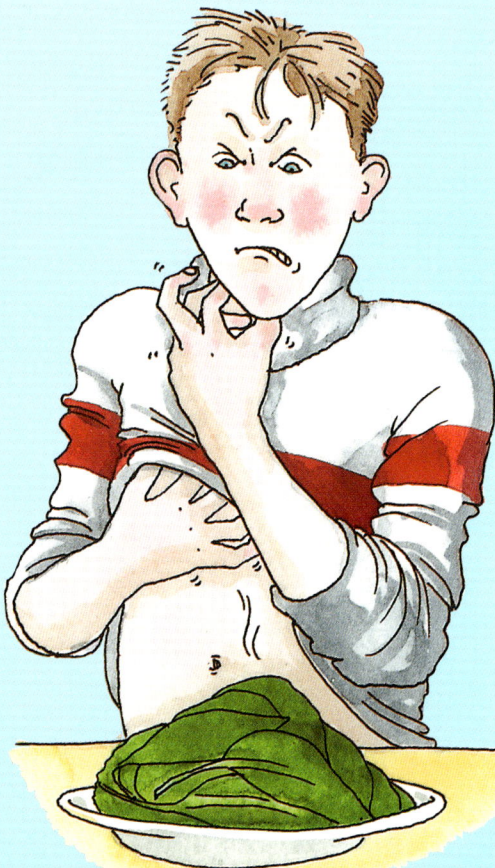

A Try to guess these jokes. (Answers at the bottom of the page.)

1. What is a frog's favourite flower?
2. What car is like a sausage?
3. What fruit is always sad?

B Can you guess any of these jokes? They are all based on place names.

1. Where do dogs learn to sing?
2. Where is the cleanest place to live?
3. Where is the best place to spend the winter?

C Make up your own jokes using these place names:

1. Cofton Hackett   2. Candy Mill
3. Little Wallop   4. Bunwell

D Make up your own 'knock, knock' joke. For example:

Knock, knock!
Who's there?
Phil.
Phil Who?
Fillet steak, please!

Answers: A 1. crocus; 2. an old banger; 3. pineapple. B 1. Barking; 2. Bath; 3. Hugglescote.

Remember A *pun* is a joke based on words that have *double meanings*.

Riddle Mee Ree

How many metaphors can you find in these riddles?

A **riddle** is a puzzle. You are given clues to work out the answer. Most riddles use **puns** or **metaphors**.

- I have the same roots as my Swedish cousin. What am I?
  A turnip (a root vegetable like a swede).

Some riddles rhyme.

A   What Am I?
My needles cannot knit or sew,
My feet are four and rather slow,
A prickly pear is all you'll see,
If danger lurks or threatens me,
My smaller friend you may well know,
That hunts by tree or green hedgerow.
What am I?

B   I am not made of cheese,
As some suppose,
A milky curve maybe,
When 'ere you doze.
What am I?

C   Now try to work out these:

1. I am a white cloud on the water.
2. I am a green jumper.
3. I show you what you think you are.
4. I am always travelling and never arriving.

D   Make up riddles for the following:

1. a pearl	**2.** an aeroplane
3. a ghost	**4.** a beaver

- Ask a partner to work them out.

Answers: A. porcupine; B. crescent moon; C. 1. swan; 2. grasshopper; 3. mirror; 4. revolving door.

Remember A *riddle* is a puzzle to be solved by the reader.

Criss-Cross

Crosswords are word puzzles:

```
c   o   m   b
        o
        m
l   a   m   b
```

You will notice that the words can be read **across** or **down**. Did you notice that all these words have **silent letters**? Most crosswords have clues.

A Copy this **homophone** crossword carefully and complete it using the clues:

Across
1. A two-letter word.
2. _____ the Looking Glass.
3. A pair.
4. Not a rabbit!

Down
1. He _____ the ball to me.
2. Belongs to us.
3. Another word for also.
4. Straight or curly?
5. Every minute counts.

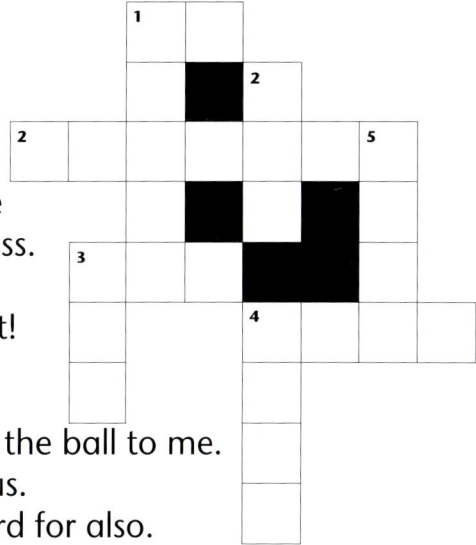

B Copy out this silent-letter crossword, putting the letters in squares. Make up Across and Down clues and do not forget to number the words and clues.

	¹k			
	n			
²k	n	i	g	h	t
	n	⬛	t	
³k	n	o	w	
	t			

- What is the silent letter in the crossword?

C Now make up your own homophone crossword using the following words. All words must be read across or down.

pear/pair   week/weak   fair/fare

Remember You can make your own *crossword* if you follow the rules.

As Fierce as a Lion

A **simile** compares something with something else by using the words:

● *like as* and *as if.*

We use similes a lot in everyday conversation. For example:

● She ran like the wind.
● He ran as swiftly as the wind.
● They ran as if their lives depended on it.

All of these refer to running very fast.

A Write down what these common similes mean:
1. As fierce as a lion.
2. As cool as cucumber.
3. As sick as a parrot.
4. As keen as mustard.
5. As clear as daylight.
6. As clear as mud.
7. As happy as Larry.
8. As bright as a button.

B Write down what you think the following mean:
1. He kept one eye open like a cat taking a nap.
2. Her voice rose, quivered and fell as if the ship would founder.
3. The day drew nearer as summer follows spring.
4. That moment long ago was like the memory of a song.

C Finish these similes using interesting ideas:
1. The dragon breathed fire like _____ .
2. The wrestler leapt into the ring like _____ .
3. Christie's bag bounced on his back like _____ .
4. The tap drip-dripped like _____ .
5. The kite floated away like _____ .

Can you finish this simile about me? As _____ as a bee!

Remember You can make a *simile* by comparing something with something else.

Smile of a Strawberry Ice Cream

A **metaphor** describes something as though it was something else:

- The delicious smile of a strawberry ice cream.

The delicious quality of the ice cream is described in terms of a smile. The metaphor does not compare it, saying it is *like* a smile. (If it did, it would be a **simile**.)

A Write down the **nouns** below and match them to the most suitable metaphors.

Nouns
a. volcano   **d.** a peppermint sweet
b. lightning   **e.** grandfather clock
c. a river   **f.** thunder

Metaphors
the crack of a whip
a plump bumble bee
the scarlet-tongued serpent
a comforting heartbeat
the blue ribbon
giant's steps

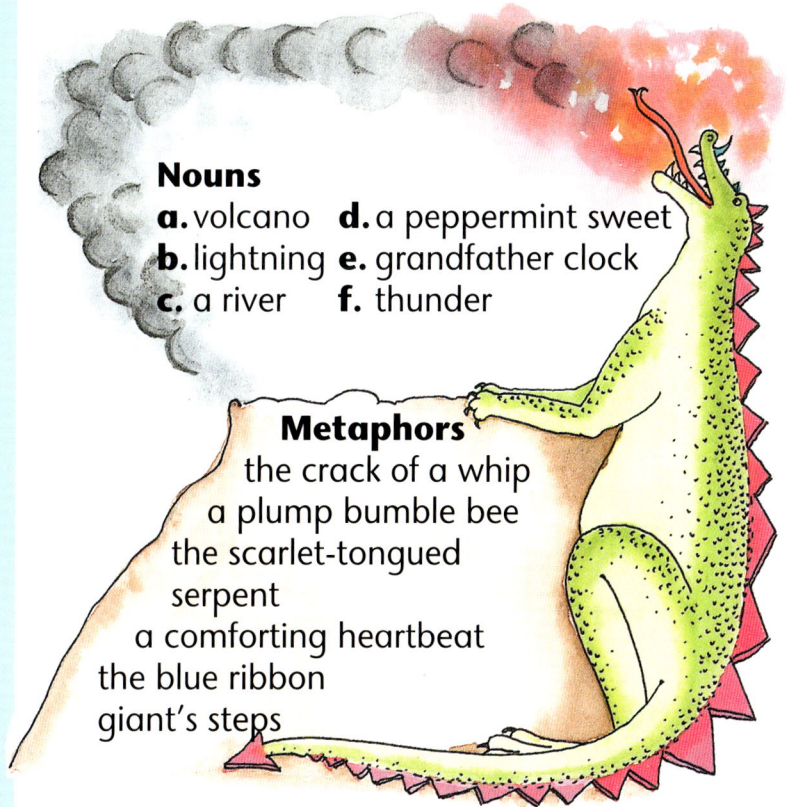

B Imagine that you are witnessing a fire. An old warehouse has caught alight. The police and fire brigade have arrived and the area is being cordoned off. The flames grow higher and higher.

- Write a description using suitable metaphors. Choose carefully and do not use too many.

Remember A *metaphor* describes something as though it is something else.

39

Dictionary Quiz

lobby lob-by [LOB-ee] *noun* **lobbies**
1. A waiting room or hall at the entrance to a hotel, a theatre, an apartment or another building.
2. A person or organised group that works to try to change the way lawmakers vote or act: *The anti-smoking lobby supported a ban on smoking in all public places.* A person who does this is a **lobbyist**. *verb,* **lobbied, lobbying** to act to change the way lawmakers vote or act: *The townspeople lobbied to have a new community centre built.*

lobster lob-ster [LOB-stur] *noun* **lobsters**
A sea animal with a hard outer shell and no backbone. **Lobsters** have five pairs of legs, with large claws on the front pair. They are often eaten as food.

local lo-cal [LOH-kul] *adjective*
Having to do with one place, especially the town or neighbourhood one lives in: *Most children go to their local school, the one closest to where they live.* A **local** area, such as a neighbourhood or town, is a **locality** or a **locale**. *noun,* **local** a person from the area. *adverb,* **locally**.

locate lo-cate [LOH-KATE *or* loh-KATE]
verb **located, locating**
1. To be or exist in a certain place: *That shop is located on the other side of the street.*
2. To put in a certain place: *They've decided to locate their new shop in the town centre.*
3. To find the position of; search out: *Once you locate the fish, you still have to catch them.*

location lo-ca-tion [loh-KAY-shun] *noun* **locations**
1. A place where something is located: *My grandparents know a perfect location for our campsite.*
2. The act of locating.
Syn: place, position, area, spot, territory, district. On **location** at a place outside the studio where a film or TV show is normally filmed: *That film was shot on location in the Rockies.*

lock[1] [lok] *noun* **locks**
1. A small device used to keep a door, window, drawer or other object closed until it is opened by a key or by some other means.
2. A part of a canal or waterway closed off with gates. The water level can be changed by letting water in or out to raise or lower boats and ships. *verb,* **locked, locking**.

1. To fasten with a lock: *Don't forget to lock the door.*
2. To shut away or hold in place: *We locked the money into the safe.*
3. To join or hold firmly in place, as if with a **lock**: *The ice locked our ship in place.*
Syn: fasten, close, latch, seal, clasp.

lock[2] *noun* **locks**
1. A piece of hair from the head.
2. **locks**. The hair of the head: *a young child with curly locks*.

locker lock-er [LOK-ur] *noun* **lockers**
A small closet or cabinet that can be locked, used for storing personal belongings in a public place.

locket lock-et [LOK-et] *noun* **lockets**
A small metal case with a picture, a lock of hair or something else that one wants to keep, usually worn on a chain around the neck.

locksmith lock-smith [LOK-SMITH] *noun* **locksmiths**
A person who makes, installs or repairs locks.

locomotive lo-co-mo-tive [LOH-kuh-MOH-tiv] *noun* **locomotives**
A railway carriage with an engine, used for pulling or pushing other carriages.

locust lo-cust [LOH-kust] *noun* **locusts**
1. A type of grasshopper that sometimes travels in huge swarms eating all the plants in its path. They can cause great damage to farm crops.
2. A tree with small, feathery leaves and sweet-smelling white flowers.

lodge [loj] *noun* **lodges**
1. A house or cottage, especially one used for a special purpose: *a fishing lodge*.
2. A branch of a larger organisation or club: *My uncle belongs to a local lodge of the Lion's Club.*
3. The den or home of an animal: a beaver's **lodge**. *verb,* **lodged, lodging**.
1. To live in a place for a time: *We lodged in a cabin near the water.*
2. To provide a place to stay: *Our friends lodged us at their place overnight.*
3. To be stuck or caught in something: *The kite lodged in the tree between two branches.*
4. To place a formal charge or complaint: *The tenants lodged a complaint about their landlord.*

Dictionary Quiz

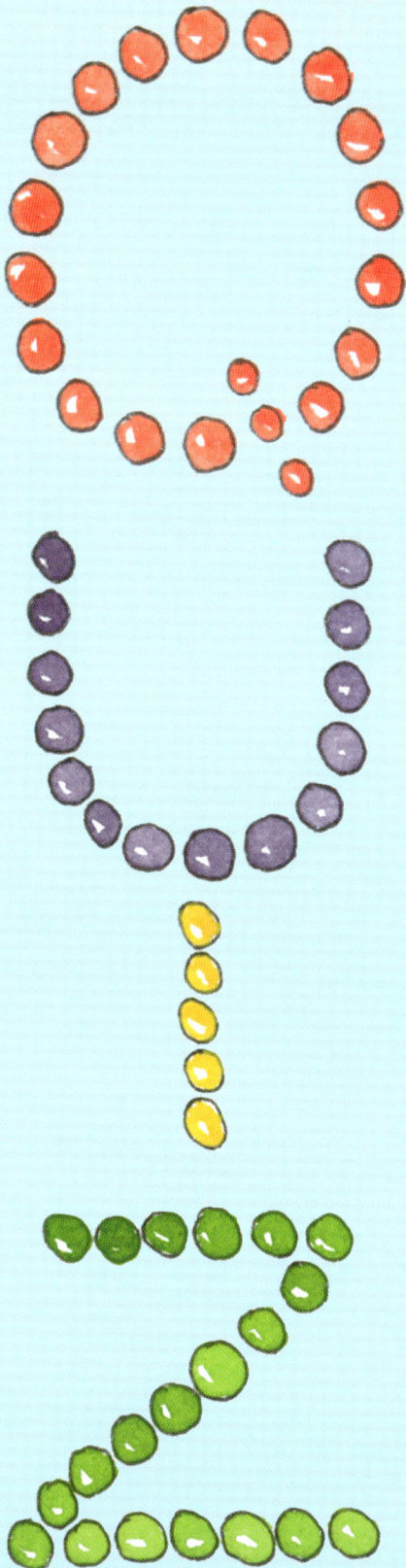

A Use the **dictionary page** on page 40 to find the answers to these questions. The words in red are called **entries**.

1. How many entries are on this page?
2. Write the word that has two entries.

An explanation of a word's meaning is called a **definition**.

3. Write the word that has the shortest definition.

When a word has more than one meaning, each definition is numbered.

4. Write the word with the most definitions.

Hyphens are used to divide **syllables**.

5. Write the first one-syllable word.
6. Write the first two-syllable word.
7. Write a three-syllable word.
8. Write a four-syllable word.

An accented syllable is written in capital letters in brackets.

9. Write the word that has two different pronunciations.
10. Write the word that has two accented syllables.

The part of speech that each word is appears in italic letters.

11. Write one **adjective**.
12. Write three **nouns** that can be both nouns and **verbs**.

The first entry on the page is 'lobby' and the last is 'lodge'. All the words fall between these two **alphabetically**.

13. Here are some nonsense words. Which could appear on this page?

loamer	lobric	loddic	locify
loody	lockance	loceful	lofant

Remember In some dictionaries each word has a pronunciation guide in brackets. Sound it out to read the correct pronunciation.

Two by Two

A These animals have arrived late for Noah's Ark. Use a **dictionary** to help you to direct them to the correct areas on the Ark.

Copy and Complete	
Animal	Classification
Turtle	Reptile

Animals	Classification
Turtle	Crustacean
Octopus	Arachnid
Salamander	Amphibian
Ant	Reptile
Frog	Insect
Scorpion	Mollusc
Clam	
Lobster	
Snake	
Spider	

Remember *Dictionaries* can give different kinds of information.

Using My Thesaurus

A **thesaurus** is a reference book. We can use it to find **synonyms** (words that have the same or similar meaning). We can also use it to find **antonyms** (words that have the opposite meaning).

Which dinosaur could play with words?

Tyrannthesaurus Rex!

fidgety
laughter
curious
secret
surprising
silence

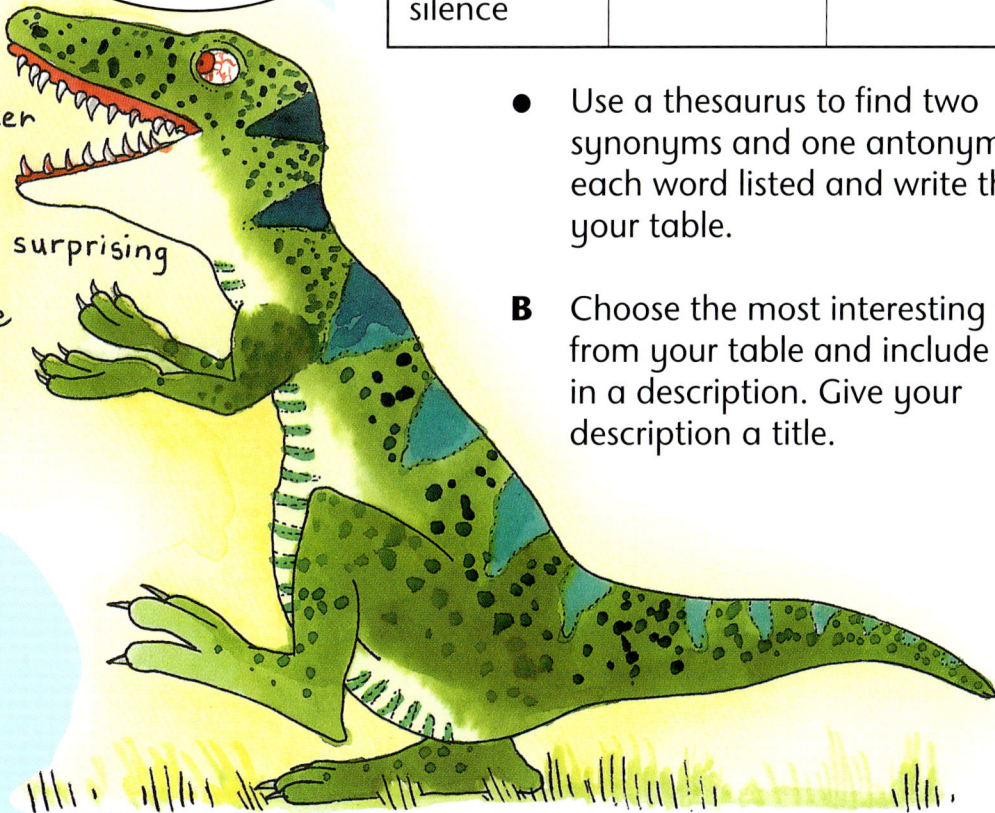

A   Draw a table in your book like this:

Copy and Complete		
Using My Thesaurus		
Word	Synonyms	Antonyms
fidgety		
laughter		
curious		
surprising		
secret		
silence		

● Use a thesaurus to find two synonyms and one antonym for each word listed and write them in your table.

B   Choose the most interesting words from your table and include them in a description. Give your description a title.

Remember You can use a *thesaurus* to find *synonyms* and *antonyms*.

Tyrone's Daily Diary

You may remember that we can write sentences in the **active** and **passive**:

● Tyrone completed the daily diary.

In the active sentence, Tyrone or the **subject** of the sentence is put first.

● The daily diary was completed by Tyrone.

In the passive sentence, what has been completed (the daily diary) or the **object** comes first.

A Find out what Tyrone and his class did that day. Then change the sentences from the active to the passive or from the passive to the active. You may need to use the word *by*.

1. Tyrone wrote up the notes from the discussion.
2. He did two pages of mathematics.
3. Five pages of a new book were read by him.
4. The class played games in the school yard.
5. A window was broken by Tommy.
6. The broken glass was cleared up by the caretaker.
7. A stray dog approached Tyrone in the playground.
8. Tyrone recognised the dog as Buster!
9. He licked Tyrone's hand.
10. Buster was taken home by Tyrone at the end of the school day.

Remember In the *active* sentence the *subject* is first.

Buster

Read the following sentence which is written in the **passive**:

● Buster was taken home *by Tyrone* at the end of the school day.

When we write in the passive we do not always use the *by* phrase:

● Buster was taken home at the end of the school day.

A Read this information about Buster, Tyrone's dog, which is written in the active. Change the first five sentences into the passive, leaving out the *by* phrase.

1. Tyrone found Buster in a dog's home.
2. He looked after the dog with great care.
3. He bought Buster a tartan collar with his name and address on it.
4. Yesterday, someone left the gate open and Buster trotted out.
5. Firstly, Buster lost his tartan collar.
6. Secondly, he _____ .
7. Thirdly, _____ .

B Finish sentences 6 and 7, and write three more sentences in the active, up to the point where Buster arrives at Tyrone's school (see page 44).

Remember We do not always need to use the *by* phrase when we write in the *passive*.

Sentence Factory

Sentences are made up of different parts.

The **subject** part tells who or what the sentence is about.

The **verb** part tells what the action is:

    subject verb

       ↓   ↓

My father picked us up.

A Copy the chart below and choose subjects that fit the category in the left-hand column. Add your own verb part.

Copy and Complete		
Category	Subject Part	Verb Part
Family member	My father	picked us up
Animal		
Machine		
Food		
Tool		
Plant		
Story character		

B Rewrite only the subject part of each of your sentences above. Add an **adjective** to each one, for example: My *thoughtful* father …

C Now go back and rewrite the verb part of each sentence. To each one, add words telling where it happened, like this:

Copy and Complete	
Subject Part	Verb Part
My *thoughtful* father	picked us up *at school*

● The verb part of a sentence is called the **predicate**.

Remember The *subject* part of a sentence tells you who or what the sentence is about. The *verb* part of a sentence tells you what happens.

Construction Company

When you want to add some detail to a sentence, you can use a group of words called a **phrase**. A phrase does not have a **verb**.

A phrase can describe something:
● *with the blue hat*

or tell when something happened:
● *in the morning*

or where something happened:
● *in a red van*

or how something happened:
● *with a loud clatter*

or which person or thing you are talking about:
● *who was left behind.*

The predicate is the verb part of a sentence.

A Write three sentences of your own using a **subject**, a **predicate** and a **phrase**.

1. _____   _____   _____
   animal   predicate   why

2. _____   _____   _____
   sports   predicate   where
   equipment

3. _____   _____   _____
   toy   predicate   when

B The sentences in the bricks below have become mixed up. Sort out the subject parts, verb parts and phrases so that they make sense.

Subjects	**Predicates** (Verb parts)	**Phrases**
1. The fiery dragon	ripened	before the game
2. My best friend	sped away from me	with a loud roar
3. All the players	called to me	down the slope
4. The strawberries	sat together	across the playground
5. My bicycle	emerged from the forest	in time for the party

Remember A *phrase* is a group of words with no *verb*. You can use it to give more detail to your sentence.

Bonfires

Another word for a sentence is a **clause**. It must have a **subject** and a **verb**:

● *The fire   glowed.*
    subject   verb

We can add a **subordinate clause** to make the sentence longer:

● The fire glowed *as dusk descended.*

A subordinate clause cannot stand alone, while the main clause can:

● *The fire glowed*
    main clause
● *as dusk descended.*
    subordinate clause

A Read the following main clauses:

> we raked the lawn
> the firelight gleamed
> the dog barked
> we piled up the leaves
> it smelled of autumn
> the twigs were dry

Now read these subordinate clauses:

> as the smoke curled upwards
> and threw them on the bonfire
> so they crackled sharply
> before it grew dark
> when he saw the flames
> while the sparks flew

● To make longer sentences combine each main clause with a suitable subordinate clause. REMEMBER: use capital letters and full stops.

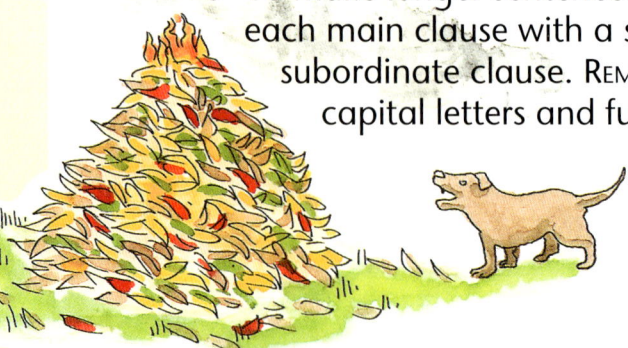

● You can place the subordinate clause first if you want to, like this: Before it grew dark, we raked the lawn.

Remember A *clause* is a sentence with a *subject* and a *verb*. The *main clause* tells you the main thing that is happening and can stand alone. The *subordinate clause* cannot stand alone.

Get It Together

A For each point below write one sentence combining all the information. This would be a **compound sentence**. For example: The tree is large. The tree has apples. The apples are green. The tree is in my garden. This could be written as: The large tree in my garden has green apples on it.

1. I was in the track event. The event was on Saturday. I ran my fastest time ever. It was the 200 metres. I won.
2. A man burst into the room. The man was tall. The man had dark hair. The man noisily threw back the door.
3. The elves made shoes. The elves lived in a tiny cottage. The cottage was on the edge of the woods. The shoes were of the finest leather.
4. We had a roadside stand. We sold lemonade. We sold cakes. We ran our stand every Saturday.
5. Katie was running. The wind blew in Katie's hair. Katie's feet clattered on the paving stones. Katie wanted to beat the rain. Katie was going home.
6. I saw a play. I went with my family. The play was in the Grand Theatre. The play was very funny.
7. I like peanut butter. Peanut butter is difficult to eat. Peanut butter can make you very sticky. I like the crunchy kind.
8. I like to swim. Swimming is good exercise. I am a good swimmer. The pool is very close to my house. I swim regularly.

Remember You can make a *compound sentence* by combining smaller sentences.

Vina's Parcel

Different **prepositions** are used in different situations:

- *During* breakfast a parcel arrived for Vina.

During is a preposition to do with **time**.

- The parcel was put *beside* Vina's chair.

Beside is a preposition to do with **position**.

- *So* she opened it immediately.

So is a preposition to do with **cause** or **reason**.

A Copy the table below.

Copy and Complete			
Time	Position	Sequence (order)	Logic (for argument or reasoning)
during	beside	after	so

- Now look at the words in the parcel and decide where they fit into your table.

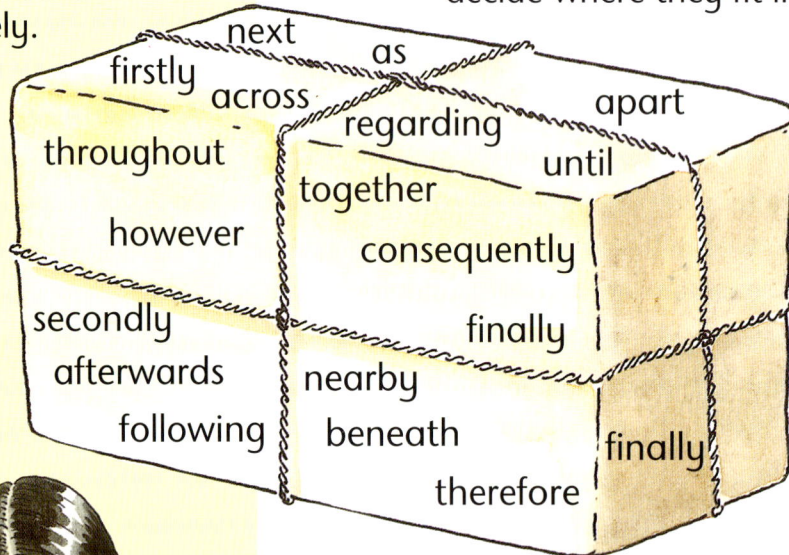

next firstly as across apart regarding throughout until together however consequently secondly finally afterwards nearby following beneath finally therefore

- Do any fit into more than one heading? Think carefully!

B Write five sentences about Vina's parcel. It contains a mysterious present. Use suitable prepositions.

C What headings would the prepositions in bold fit into?
1. **under** the circumstances
2. **under** the table
3. **while** he was out
4. **while** I agree

Remember Different *prepositions* are used in different situations.

Dean's Bike

A **colon** is a pause often used to list information or give an explanation:

- He bought: two kilos of carrots, a bunch of watercress and three vegetable samosas.

- At the top of the form was written: Complete the following using black ink.

However, colons are also used in scriptwriting.

A Read the following:

1. Dean is delivering newspapers and has propped his bike against a wall.
P.C. Percy: Hullo, Hullo, Hullo!
Dean: *(muttering to himself)* Oh no!
P.C. Percy: Is this your bike, lad?
(Dean's mouth is open but nothing comes out.)
P.C. Percy: No back light, no front light, no bell. Tyres unroadworthy, mudguards falling off ... what have we here, then?
Dean: _____

- Complete the script, putting the colons in the right place.

- Why do you think colons are used in scripts?

B How many colons have been used on this page? Look carefully!

Remember *Colons* are used in scriptwriting.

Joining the Parts

We can show that two ideas or bits of information are closely linked by using a **semicolon**.

● Melody read the detective novel from cover to cover; she was a voracious reader.

The second part of the sentence gives us additional information about Melody as a reader. Note that you do not need a capital letter after a semicolon.

A Pair sentences **1** to **5** with **6** to **10** in the most suitable way. Write them out using a semicolon. REMEMBER: you do not need a capital letter after the semicolon.

1. All the birds suddenly flew out of the maple tree.
2. The project was completely finished.
3. He could not remember where he had put the file.
4. The underside of the car was rusty.
5. She loved candyfloss and toffee apples.

6. It was typical that this should happen.
7. It had been a long time in the making.
8. They reminded her of her childhood.
9. They were like rushing water.
10. It had certainly seen better days.

B Write two sentences of your own using semicolons.

What does the prefix 'semi' mean? Think of three more words that use it.

The Mystery of the Missing Semicolon

Remember A *semicolon* shows that two ideas are closely linked.

Leaving Messages

The **dash** can be used in several ways. Sometimes we use it rather like a **comma**. It can be a pause that separates two parts of a statement. We often use it when we want to write quickly; when we leave out words because we only want to give basic information.

If we take a message we often use dashes:

Telephone Messages

Uncle Joe called — 11am — please ring back about the tickets — wants three

3pm — Uncle Joe rang — wants four tickets

Uncle Joe again — 5pm — please ring before 6pm

A The dashes have been left out from the following messages. Write them out correctly.

1. Mum says put the fish plaice and cod in the freezer.
2. Salad in the fridge keys in the top drawer.
3. Sabre has been fed needs walkies.
4. Sameera rang meet outside cinema 7p.m.

B Sameera rings three more times, changing the arrangements and also adding new information. You take the messages. Write them down using dashes.

When is a dash not a dash?

When it's a slowcoach!

Remember A *dash* is rather like a *comma* but is often used when we want to write quickly.

A Winning Streak

Brackets surround information that is set apart from the rest of the sentence. Without this information the sentence should still make sense:

● He looks happy compared to the last time I saw him (about two months ago) and is clearly on the road to recovery.

Read the sentence without the information in the brackets. What do you notice?

Brackets can also be used when we make a **reference** to something:

● Danny O'Reilly (see picture below) is the happy winner of our summer competition!

A Write out these sentences, putting the brackets in the correct places:

1. Danny, my brother's friend he lives on the other side of town won a competition last week.
2. He is allowed to take a friend as well as his family for a two-week holiday all costs included on a Caribbean cruise.
3. My brother Philip his nickname's Pip could hardly believe his luck when Danny invited him on the cruise.
4. Mum said we could all visit the liner it's docked in Southampton when Pip is due to leave.
5. My older sister said she would buy Pip a camera an automatic one to take on holiday.

B Decide where the brackets go in these sentences. Write down why.

1. Please complete the form see p.8 and return it to the address given.
2. You will need several pieces of equipment Fig. 1.
3. Her first book 1985 was written when she was thirty-two.

Remember *Brackets* can be used to surround information set apart from the rest of the sentence.

Take a Letter

We change the way we write according to the person we are writing to or **addressing**:

● Dear Sir,
   Thank you for your letter of September 8th concerning your request. Forms may be obtained from ...

● Dear Polly,
   Thanks for your letter. It was good to hear from you again ...

The first letter is written as if we did not know the person we were addressing. It is a **formal** letter which has an **impersonal** tone. It uses expressions such as *your letter of* and *concerning your request.* The second is friendly. It has a **personal** tone. The expressions are casual, as if we were talking to the person.

A Make two headings: **formal** and **informal**.

● Write the following under the correct headings:

1. An e-mail to a friend.
2. A letter of complaint.
3. A letter of thanks to your auntie.
4. A birthday card.
5. An application for a job.
6. Requesting an appointment at a clinic.
7. Thanking a stranger for returning your lost dog.
8. A holiday postcard.

B You have written for membership forms to join a club. (Choose a club related to your interests such as a fan club or a football club.) Write the reply you receive, giving you instructions about what to do. Use the following impersonal expressions:
● Forms may be obtained from –
● I would like to draw your attention to –
● Regarding the –
● – by return of post.

Remember When we write a *formal* letter we use an *impersonal* tone.

Diwali

When we want to find out about a topic we need to select the most important points for our purpose. To do this we can **make notes**. It is best to carry out our research in stages.

A Andy and his group are doing a project on Hinduism. He needs to find out some **facts** about Diwali. Follow the stages and write suitable notes that Andy can read.

1. First, have some idea about what you need to find out:
   Diwali – When held? For how long? What does it mean? What happens?

2. Read the information through:

   Diwali, the festival of lights, is the most important festival in the Hindu calendar. It is held in Ashwin which is during September and October and usually lasts between three and five days. Diwali cards are sent and sweets are made from milk, honey and coconut. Everybody enjoys themselves but the festival also has an important message – that goodness can triumph. Diwali means 'a row of lights' and the light is a symbol of goodness. Hundreds of arti lamps are lit and fireworks are set off. Beautiful rangoli patterns are drawn on the ground and stories about the gods are told.

3. Select the most important facts which answer your questions. Use key words like this:
   When held? **Ashwin** – Sept/Oct

● Now complete the notes you will give Andy, making sure he can read them. Add any extra facts you think are important.

Remember You should have some idea about what you need to find out before *making notes*.

Rama and Sita

Sometimes you need to sum up a topic or story. This means you need to write down the **main points** as a short account or **summary**.

You can also use notes to write a summary.

A Read the following story about Rama and Sita:

Prince Rama had a beautiful wife called Sita. They lived blissfully together until one day the cruel Ravana, King of the Demons, who had ten pairs of arms and ten heads, carried Sita away.

Rama was distraught. He did not know what to do. But Hanuman the monkey god discovered where Sita was. She had been imprisoned in Ravana's fortress on the island of Lanka.

So, Hanuman and his monkey soldiers worked to free Sita. They built a bridge that spanned the sea from India to Lanka and together Rama, Hanuman and his monkey army crossed over to fight the demon king.

The battle was long and bloodthirsty until at last Rama struck Ravana with his magic arrow made of fire and sunlight. Sita was rescued and they all returned to India. Since then the story of Rama and Sita is told each year at Diwali, the festival of lights.

● Write down the main points in each paragraph. Use key words like this:

Para 1. **Sita,** Prince Rama's wife, **is carried away** by **Ravana**.
Para 2. _____

● Turn the main points into sentences, **summarising** the story.

B Use the notes you made about Diwali on page 56 and write another summary.

Remember A *summary* is a short account containing the *main points* of a topic or story.

Magazines

There are several things you can do to improve your work. One of these is to **edit** it. This means you should remove any words that are not needed. Read this example of unedited text:

- Before a book is published it is edited. This book has been edited.

After the text has been edited, it may read like this:

- Before a book, such as this one, is published, it is edited.

A Read the following two paragraphs and edit them. REMEMBER: remove *only* unwanted words and phrases. Try to ensure that the paragraphs flow easily.

Magazines seem to fill the shelves of newsagents, supermarkets and 24-hour stores. There are more and more being produced for every conceivable interest – from A – astronomy, to Z – zoology. What's your hobby? You can be sure there's a magazine about it. The range of these publications, in style and layout, is awesome, but so is competition and many that you see on the shelves today will be gone tomorrow.

Of course, catering for a particular interest is not new. Magazines have been with us for many years. They have been with us in a simple form since the eighteenth century. The word 'magazine' originally meant 'store' and the title of a book frequently contained the word 'magazine' to show it was a book that provided particular information.

B Write a third paragraph about the magazines you and your family read, then edit it.

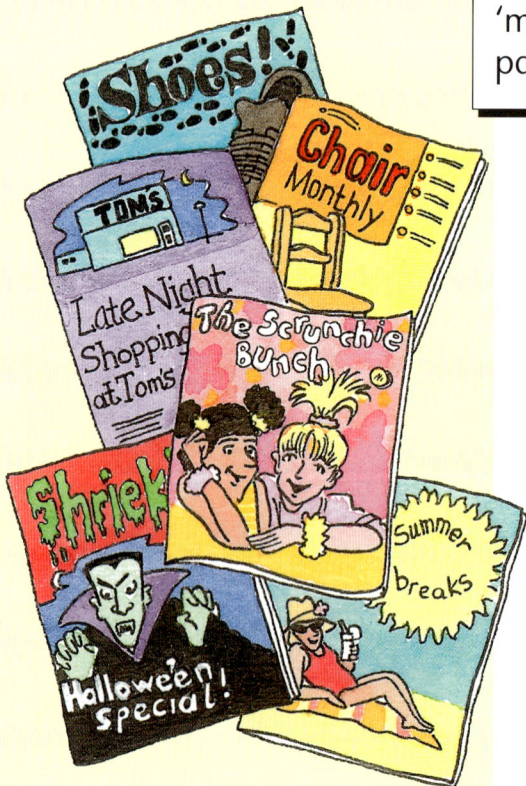

What else does 'magazine' mean? How does this link to its original meaning?

Remember When you *edit*, you remove words that are not needed.

Dear Simone

When we check our work to find out where the mistakes are, we **proofread** it.

Special symbols are used for proofreading. Some of these are shown below.

spelling mistake	sp
new paragraph	//
capital letter	≡
punctuation mistake	p
new sentence	/
full stop	ʘ

A Read Lucy's letter and write it out again, leaving a space between each line. Use symbols to proofread it. Then redraft it, adding the date and address. There are 20 mistakes! Can you find them all? REMEMBER: use all the symbols.

Dear Simone,

Thank you for your letter. You've been to paris, have you. I wish I'd been with you nothing exciting has happened here, but there has been one silly insident. I'm always forgeting phone numbers and addresses I write them on scraps of paper, put them in my pocket or in my bag and lose them. So, my older brother, dave, bought me an address book. It's loose-leaf and you can add pages to it and of course its in affabetical order. I spent all day yesterday organising it. I wrote in your address my school friends addresses and Auntie Jane's new address in hollywood. I also included addresses such as the doctors and the dentist's When I'd finished I left the book on the kitchen table. Foolish. Timmy, my three-year old brother, thought he would investigate He pulled out all the pages, creased them up and gave them to the cat to play with! So I'm back to sqare one.

write and tell me your news again.

Your penpal,

Lucy

What did the robber say to the policeman?

Proof it!

Remember You can check your work by *proofreading* it.

Check Again

- It is important for your final draft to be as perfect as you can make it. You will need to **proofread** it to make sure you have no mistakes.

A Read this story. Then follow the instructions on the next page to help you to proofread the story.

Once upon a time in the 11 century there lived a pirate named Blackbeard. Blackbeard was one of the most pirates ever to sale the seven seas. One day Blackbeard and his shipmates were on the shore, they heard from someone that there was a treasure buried on an Island call 'Danger Island' immediately Blackbeard and his crew mates went to find the treasure. They all went in their ship to sil to the Island, but when they arrived the ship was kind of stuck to the water it was so sticky just like tar but they some how managed to make it. They all had arrived on the island safe and sound but not for long they entered cave that had an aero pointing inside Blackbeard lit a match to see where they were the map said walk up 50 metres to the West and then 20 metres to the North but suudenly out of nowhere the ground was opened up and Blackbeard and his shipmates had fell into the hole. They all woke up to find themselves ina swamp they all swam to shore everyone was all right but the map was all wet and the ink was running, uphead there was a sign that said 'BEWARE' and the shipmates were afraid and said lets go back but Blackbeard was not and yelled follow me so they had entered into another cave when they saw the tresure and they all jumped for joy.

Remember Be a *proofreader* and make your final draft as good as it can be.

Check Again (continued)

A Copy the story exactly as it appears on page 60, then correct it, following the instructions below, using a red pen. Leave a space between each line so that you can write above the text. Refer to the proofreading correction marks on page 59.

1. Read the story again and make sure there is a **capital letter** at the beginning and a **full stop** at the end of every sentence.
2. Find all the names of people and things (**proper nouns**) and make sure they start with capital letters. Make sure the **common nouns** start with lower case letters.
3. Check the story to make sure that whenever a **homophone** is used it is the correct one.
4. Put in all the **quotation marks** you think are needed.
5. Read the story again and put in any words that have been left out.
6. Check that new paragraphs begin in the correct place.
7. Look for any **contractions** or **possessive words** that are missing an **apostrophe**.
8. Read the story again, and put in any missing **commas**.
9. Check one last time, and correct any spelling errors you find.
10. Now, write a final draft of the story on another piece of paper, correcting all the errors you found.
11. Ask someone to check your rewritten version to make sure you have not missed anything.

● The next time you **proofread** your own writing, check through it more than once. Look for a different kind of error each time as you did here.

Remember It's important to learn to *proofread* your work for errors.

Double Consonants

Many two-syllable words have **double consonants** in the middle:

*pu**dd**le   bu**tt**er   bo**bb**in.*

A   Write out the missing word from these **proverbs**. Guess the word if you do not know it. Explain what the proverbs mean.

1. A ro____ stone gathers no moss.
2. Great oaks from li____ acorns grow.
3. Fine words bu____ no parsnips.
4. Be____ late than never.
5. A bad workman qua____ with his tools.

B   Write out the following, adding double consonants to complete the word. Make two words for each one, using different consonants. Choose from these consonants:

> **bb dd ff gg ll mm nn pp rr ss tt**

a. ra__ __le	**b.** su__ __er	**c.** ri__ __le
d. wa__ __le	**e.** se__ __er	**f.** ru__ __er
g. bo__ __le	**h.** co__ __on	**i.** bi__ __er
j. ho__ __er	**k.** le__ __er	**l.** shu__ __er

● Record any words with double letters that you are unsure of.

Remember Many two-syllable words have *double consonants* in the middle.

A Muddle Up

There are many spellings which we muddle up. These are often words that sound the same (**homophones**) or words that sound similar. For example:

- *to too two*
- *as has.*

A Write out these sentences, choosing the correct homophone from the words in the brackets. Read the sentences first to make sure you understand them.

1. Dad put (*to/too/two*) much in Kevin's lunch box: eight sandwiches, three bananas (*to/too/two*) apples and a (*pair/pear*).
2. Jordan (*as/has*) taken the wrong (*pair/pear*) of socks again!
3. "The children have been asked to wait with (*their/there/they're*) pets in the corner, over (*their/there/they're*)," explained Mrs Flowers, crossly.
4. "All I want is (*to/too/two*) put my feet up, have a cup of tea and some (*piece/peace*) and (*quite/quiet*)," said Mum with a yawn.
5. For some reason, Lenny always (*read/red*) *Jack and the* (*Beenstalk/Beanstalk*) each evening to his three-year-old brother.
6. "(*Wear/Where*) on earth do you think you've (*been/bean*)? – it's seven o'clock!" demanded Mum.
7. It was Sunday evening, rainy and dull, and the children were (*bored/board*).
8. Mr Potter was (*find/fined*) for leaving his car on a double yellow line.
9. "Come (*ear/here/hear*), look what I've found!" called Tina, and she placed the shell to her (*ear/here/hear*).
10. Simon (*knew/new*) his gran would (*buy/by*) him a (*knew/new*) bike, but he (*thought/fought*) it was rude to ask.

Remember Record any spellings you often confuse.

Checking Punctuation

You should have a good understanding of when to use a:

- **full stop**   .
- **capital letter**   A B C
- **question mark**   ?
- **exclamation mark** !
- **comma**   ,

A   There is more than one **punctuation** mistake in each of the following statements. Write them out correctly.

1. do you always forget to spend your pocket money
2. Each morning even when it rains I take Bess for a walk
3. My goodness We thought you would never arrive in time for the pantomime
4. how often does your father visit his allotment
5. The donkey whose name was percy loved crunching apples.
6. watch out The paint tin is about to topple over!
7. Did you know that dina my sister had won the snooker championship?
8. He bought a beautiful model boat for Dilip to sail on the pond
9. Whoosh Annie her arms flying out sped down the helter-skelter at top speed.
10. you can fly the kite on the village green tomorrow afternoon

Remember Make sure you can use basic *punctuation*.

The Verb 'To Be'

Some **verbs** express an action you can see, such as *run* or *dive*.

Some verbs express actions and thoughts you cannot see, like *hope* or *dream*.

The verb *to be* is a special verb. It tells what someone or something is:

● I *am* a student. You *are* a student too. It *is* a long way to school.

Listed below are other ways that you can use the verb *to be*.

I am	he is
she is	it is
we are	you are
they are	I was
he was	she was
it was	we were
you were	they were
I will be	he will be
she will be	it will be
you will be	they will be

A Write a sentence using the verb *to be* to answer each of these questions. The first one is started for you.

Copy and Complete

1. How many pupils are in your class?
There are _____ .

1. How many pupils are in your class?
2. Who is the oldest person in your family?
3. How old will he or she be next birthday?
4. How old were you on your last birthday?
5. What kind of creature was Winnie the Pooh?
6. What colour are the shoes you are wearing?
7. How would you describe the weather today?
8. Would you describe yourself as a good athlete?
9. In your opinion, what is the best story you have ever read?
10. What do you think will be the most interesting thing you do next week?

Remember The verb *to be* is special – it tells you what someone or something is. It can be written in the past, present or future.

Irregular Past Tenses

To write most **verbs** in the past tense you add **ed**:

- "Yesterday I *walked* to school."

Some verbs do not follow this pattern. They are called **irregular**:

- "This morning I *ran* to school because I was late."

A There are 22 irregular past-tense verbs in this wordsearch. Write each one that you find beside its present-tense partner. If you need to circle the words as you find them, carefully copy the wordsearch first.

b	r	o	u	g	h	t	o	w
r	o	d	e	w	r	o	t	e
o	c	u	t	o	h	i	d	r
k	s	g	h	n	c	a	m	e
e	m	g	o	t	h	r	e	w
l	e	d	u	s	h	o	n	e
c	a	u	g	h	t	s	o	n
e	t	g	h	s	p	e	n	t
s	e	n	t	a	u	g	h	t

dig	lead	cut
are	go	break
write	ride	hide
bring	send	win
eat	throw	catch
teach	spend	get
shine	come	think
rise		

- For example: dig ⟶ dug.

B Write out any other irregular past-tense verbs you can think of for future reference.

Remember An *irregular* past-tense *verb* is one that is not formed by adding the ending **ed**.

A New Beginning

You can vary the sentences in your writing by starting with an **adverb**. This can set the picture for your reader very quickly.

A Finish each of these sentences. You will notice that there is a **comma** after each adverb, to show a slight pause before the rest of the sentence.

Copy and Complete
1. Tenderly, Janice lifted the newborn puppy from the basket.

1. Tenderly, _____ .

2. Slowly, _____ .

3. Eagerly, _____ .

4. Rapidly, _____ .

5. Finally, _____ .

6. Loudly, _____ .

7. Frantically, _____ .

8. Dejectedly, _____ .

9. Happily, _____ .

10. Wisely, _____ .

11. Menacingly, _____ .

12. Amazingly, _____ .

13. Smoothly, _____ .

B Add five more sentences starting with adverbs. Put a comma after your opening adverb.

Remember You can use *adverbs* to start sentences.

Adjectives

Adjectives make your writing more interesting, because they give your reader details.

A Look at the sentences below describing a day out. Use more interesting and exciting adjectives to replace the adjectives in these sentences. Write at least three new adjectives for each sentence. For example:

1. It was a nice day.
It was an <u>exciting, brilliant, fantastic</u> day!

1. It was a nice day.

2. The bus was full.

3. The children were pleased.

4. Lunch was good.

5. We played fun games.

6. We got wet in the rain.

7. We agreed the day had been a good one.

B Now write a short story about what you did at the weekend, using as many of the adjectives from your sentences as you can.

Remember When you are writing, vary the *adjectives* you use and choose ones which are interesting and exciting.

Connectives

Remember that **connectives**, such as **prepositions**, link two parts of a sentence. You can use them to make a sentence longer:

● I gobbled up my tea.
● I gobbled up my tea *after* I had been swimming.

A Write out the following sentences, using connectives from the box to link each pair. Choose which fits best like this: The garden gnome winked at us *as* we walked up the path. Use each connective once only.

while	before	though
as	beside	so	since

1. The garden gnome winked at us. We walked up the path.
2. Julie and Ali refused to collect the deckchairs from the shed. I asked them twice.
3. The bees buzzed among the marigolds. The stream at the bottom of the garden.
4. The cat slept in the tree. The baby slept in his pram.
5. We cleared away the toys. We carried the picnic basket onto the lawn.
6. I had jelly and ice cream. There was no trifle left.
7. Julie and Ali played tennis during the whole picnic. Mum was cross.

Remember You can use *connectives* to make your sentences longer. *Prepositions* are connectives.

Spelling

A The account below contains 12 spelling mistakes which are written in bold. Write out each spelling mistake correctly.

News Travels Fast

At **won** time this statement was true only for the **locle** area in which you lived. Most news was **scent** by word of mouth or by letter. To send information further **afeild** you would need to employ a messenger who travelled by horse. A **mesage** might take days, **weaks** or even **munths** to reach its destination. **Tuday**, news is flashed all around the world by **televishun** and radio. Satellites orbit the **erth** sending pictures and **fone** calls. News in the morning may **allready** be out of date by the afternoon.

Homophones

Homophones are words that sound the same, but have different spellings and different meanings. When you are trying to decide which homophone to use, think of other words that have similar meanings.

A Each box below holds members of two word families. Sort the words into two groups by putting together words with related meanings.

1. chord
cord
chorus
cordless
choir
choral

2. there's
theirs
here's
ours
where's
yours
mine

3. side
sighed
outside
sighing
inside
sigh
sideways

4. cent
sent
century
send
centimetre
sender
sending

5. here   hearing
hear   there
somewhere   heard
overheard   nowhere

6. berry   bury
buried   strawberry
raspberry   burying
burial   blueberry

Remember Learn the meanings of *homophones* to remember their spellings.

Direct Speech

When we write **direct speech** we use **speech marks** because we are writing down what was actually spoken.

A Can you imagine a conversation between your toothbrush and your teeth? Would it be friendly? Would they argue?
Choose two of these pairs, and write a conversation they might have.

> toothbrush and teeth
> hammer and nail
> mountain bike and mountain
> hair and comb
> pen and paper
> radio and television

● Points to remember:
– Use a comma before the speech marks, if it is not the beginning of the sentence.
– Put all your end punctuation inside the speech marks.
– Start each new speech on a new line:
 He called, "Will you wait for us?"
 "Hurry up, then!" she replied.

Remember When you write *direct speech* use the correct punctuation and start each new speech on a new line.

Reported Speech

When we write **reported speech** we do not use **speech marks** because we are not speaking directly. We are reporting what happened:

- **Direct speech**: "I can't hold this spaghetti much longer!" said the fork, in desperation.
- **Reported speech**: The fork, in desperation, said that it could not hold the spaghetti much longer.

A Read the following conversation between a knife and fork. Write it in reported speech. You will need to change the order of words and may also need to add some, but you should not change the meaning.

"What's the matter with you?" asked the fork.
"I feel useless," said the knife mournfully.
"Useless? Why?" continued the fork.
"Because this spaghetti has told me I'm not needed," moaned the knife. "It's told me to go away!"
"Well, you're certainly not as important as me," replied the fork. "Just watch me deal with him."
"You're no better than me," laughed the knife, as the spaghetti wriggled away and the fork looked bewildered.
"I have to admit he's a slippery customer," the fork sighed, "but unless we get the better of him, the spoon will take centre stage!"

B Now change the conversation you wrote on page 72 from direct to reported speech.

Remember *Reported speech* tells or *reports* what has already happened. It does not use *speech marks*.

The Apostrophe (1)

When we shorten words we use an **apostrophe**:

- *they'll* (they will)
- *let's* (let us).

A The following dialogue sounds clumsy because it has no shortened words. It does not sound like normal conversation. Write out the dialogue, using the apostrophe to shorten words.

April Fool

Ticket Inspector:	Tickets please!
Passenger:	Certainly, it is here.
Ticket Inspector:	No, that is the wrong date.
Passenger:	The wrong date. It is not, is it ?
Ticket Inspector:	I am afraid so.
Passenger:	You mean I do not have the right ticket?
Ticket Inspector:	Yes, that is wrong, you have the right ticket. I mean, no, you are right, you have the wrong ticket. I mean ... yes ... .
Passenger:	You mean I have got the wrong ticket ...?
Ticket Inspector:	Well, I mean ... sorry sir ... I mean ... we will have to take your name and address.
Passenger:	You will have to take my name and address?!
Ticket Inspector:	_____ .

B Now read through the conversation again and complete it using shortened words. (Note the title of the conversation.)

Remember When we shorten words we use the *apostrophe*.

The Apostrophe (2)

You may remember that we use the **apostrophe** to show that something belongs to someone or something:

● The *horse's* stable was full of hay.
(the stable *belonging to* the horse).

Remembering where the apostrophe goes when we are talking about something belonging to a **plural** often causes problems:

● The *horses'* stable was full of hay.
(the stable *belonging to* the horses).

When the plural has no **s** and needs an apostrophe we treat the plural as though it were **singular**.

● The *men's* job was to feed the horses.
(the job *belonging to* the men).

A Write out the following passage, making sure the apostrophes are in the correct places:

City Farm

Piglets, calves, lambs, chicks and foals could be found on the City Farm which had been built on one of the councils derelict sites. There was also an old carthorse, a bull and a pets corner. The animals homes were tailor-made and the farms location was ideal. Many of the citys children visited regularly. Now it was to be closed and the land redeveloped. A shopping mall was to take the City Farms place. But the developers had not foreseen the reaction. Childrens protest groups sprang up everywhere _____ .

B Now finish the account.

Remember The *apostrophe* showing ownership can change its position.

Synonyms

What is the difference between being *alone* and being *lonely*? These words mean almost the same thing, but we use them to express slightly different situations.

● *Tap* on a door. *Knock* on a door. *Thump* on a door.

What is the difference?

Words that mean almost the same thing are called **synonyms**. Choosing just the right synonym can help you to make your writing more interesting.

A Write out the sentences below and choose one of the suggested synonyms to complete the blank in each statement.

1. They managed to stop the sledge right on the _____ of the cliff.
   (*margin, edge, rim, brink*)
2. Billy the Kid was a _____ outlaw in days gone by. (*famous, notorious*)
3. We can grab a _____ lunch before we have to leave for school. (*fast, hasty*)
4. You have left us with a _____ problem to solve. (*heavy, weighty*)
5. Riding through that stony terrain might _____ your tyres.
   (*injure, harm, hurt, damage*)
6. They came upon an _____ castle hidden among the trees.
   (*ancient, obsolete, antique*)
7. The archaeologists had only a tiny _____ of skull to study.
   (*portion, piece, section, fragment*)
8. We all gathered at the _____ of our new clubhouse.
   (*place, position, location, spot, site*)
9. The conspirators hatched a cunning _____ . (*plan, plot, project*)
10. Sheena and Julie displayed their winning science fair project with _____ .
    (*pride, vanity, arrogance*)

● If you want information about synonyms and what they mean, you can look in a **thesaurus**.

Remember Words that have similar meanings are called *synonyms*.

Nouns

Remember:

- a **common noun** is the name of a:
  person   place   thing
  boy   sandpit bucket

- a **proper noun** is a special name:
  Jake
  The Houses of Parliament

- we use **pronouns** to replace other nouns:
  I me you we she they her his it its ours

- a **collective noun** refers to a group:
  herd   bunch

- a noun which describes a feeling or condition is called an **abstract noun**:
  happiness   beauty.

A   Read the following. Some nouns are highlighted.

> **Surjit** was a spectacular **footballer**. She practised regularly and played for **her** school **team**, Pippington Primary. Everybody would attend her matches each **Saturday**. The crowd would cheer, the **children** would throw their scarves in the air and wave **banners**. Their **belief** in her always boosted Surjit's **confidence** and she would send the **ball** to the back of the net without fail!

Draw a table like this:

Copy and Complete				
Nouns				
common	proper	pronoun	collective	abstract

- Write the nouns in the passage that are highlighted in bold under the correct heading. Can you find any more nouns? Add them to the table.

Remember There are several types of *noun*.

77

Pronouns: I and Me

Pronouns are words that are used to replace **nouns**. The proper noun *Rachel* could be replaced by the pronoun *she* or *her*. *Tim* could be replaced by *he* or *him*.

It is important to use the pronouns *I* and *me* correctly. When you add other people, remember that the rest of your sentence should not change. Read these pairs of sentences:

● I went on holiday.
My family and I went on holiday.

● Mum brought home a puppy for me.
Mum brought home a puppy for *my sister and me.*

A The pronouns below have been highlighted in bold. Write which word or words you think each one replaces.

It was **our** chance to score a goal, so I kicked the ball to Sarah and she kicked it to Ravi. **He** played it into the other team's end, but **they** brought **it** back out.

B Rewrite each of these sentences, adding a phrase bringing in other people. The first one is done for you.

Copy and Complete

1. I ran all the way.
James and I ran all the way.

1. I ran all the way.
2. I will pick you up at 8 o'clock.
3. The bus stopped for me.
4. I stepped gingerly through the doorway.
5. Silently, I descended the staircase.
6. The parcel was addressed to me.
7. The book belongs to me.
8. If you want, I will post it for you on the way home.
9. You can come with me to the game on Saturday.

● If you are not sure when to use *I* and when to use *me*, just think of the sentence without the other people.

Remember Make sure you know how to use *I* and *me* correctly.

Punctuation

- The account below is about how myths and legends began.

A The highlighted section has some punctuation missing. Read the whole account. Write out the highlighted section so that it is clear, putting in the following punctuation:

- **capital letters**
- **full stops**
- **question marks**
- **commas.**

Myths and Legends

Today we know a great deal about how the natural world works. We have explanations for rainfall, for thunder and lightning. We know how animals and plants are reproduced. Long ago, early cultures did not have scientific explanations for these things. Their knowledge of weather and life around them was different from our own. They believed that such a powerful force as, for example, the sun, must be the work of a god. Stories and poems grew about the power of the spirit world. We call these stories myths and legends.

all cultures have their own myths, but certain types of stories appear again and again. Can you guess what one of these could be It is the creation myth the story of how the world began. For the Native Americans the world was begun by a raven who dropped stones into the sea and made land. for the Norse people the gods made the world from the giant ymir they used his blood to make the sea his flesh to make the earth and his bones to make mountains. there are hundreds of creation myths How many do you know

---

Parts of Words

Recognising common **prefixes** and **suffixes** and splitting words into **syllables** will help you to spell difficult words. For example:

- exhaustion
  ex-haus-tion
- exhibition
  ex-hib-i-tion.

Making a **mnemonic** for the part of the word you often get wrong can also help. For example:

- ex**hib**ition
  hats **in** **b**loom.

A Match words that have the same prefixes and write them down. Now do the same with those that have the same suffixes. Some words may appear in both lists.

incredible	approval	illumination
survival	expenditure	imagination
literature	disorderly	receipt
impossible	discontinue	incomplete
recommend	removal	surveyor

- Make sure you understand the meaning of the words.

B Split the words into their syllables and learn to spell them. Make up mnemonics for the parts of the words you get wrong.

Remember Recognising *suffixes* and *prefixes*, splitting words into *syllables* and making *mnemonics* can help you to spell better.

Meaning and Spelling

Knowing the **meaning** of words will help you to spell them more easily. It will also help you to distinguish between words that are often confused. For example:

- *diary* – a book which records dates and daily events
- *dairy* – a building where milk is extracted and processed.

A Write out these words with the correct definition (meaning). Look up in a dictionary those you do not know. See how many you remember in a couple of days. Then check their spellings.

> stationery/stationary   excess/access
> principle/principal   emission/omission
> dependant/dependent

1. too much; an amount of something that is more than needed
2. first in order of importance
3. the means of gaining entrance to a place or to something
4. (**noun**) a person who relies on someone else
5. not moving; still
6. a rule or belief which people live by
7. writing materials and equipment
8. a discharge of something such as gas
9. (**adjective**) requiring someone or something for support
10. someone or something that has been left out

B Check the meanings of: 'practise' and 'practice', 'effect' and 'affect'.

Remember Knowing the *meaning* of words can help you to recall their spellings.

Subject and Verb

You may remember that a sentence is a **clause** and must have a **subject** and a **verb**:

- The powerful *motorbike*
  subject
  screeched to a halt.
  verb

A Make a table like the one below.

Copy and Complete	
Subject	Verb

- Read these sentences and decide which is the subject and which is the verb. Write them on your table.

  1. The traffic rumbled along monotonously.
  2. Rain dripped from umbrellas.
  3. Exhaust fumes lingered.
  4. The traffic lights faltered again.
  5. A driver beeped his horn in irritation.
  6. Then, surprisingly, the sun appeared.
  7. All at once, umbrellas closed.
  8. Children in wellington boots splashed in puddles.
  9. Dogs out walking wagged their tails.
  10. The high street pavements thronged with activity.

B Write three more sentences about the high street. Underline the subjects and verbs.

Remember Try to recognise the *subject* and *verb* in a sentence.

The Main Clause

Remember that a **clause** is a simple sentence. It makes sense on its own:

● The sweet shop was popular.

The **main clause** in a longer sentence is like a simple sentence. It also makes sense on its own and is the main point in the sentence:

● *The sweet shop*, which had served the town for years, *was popular* with all the children.

A Identify the main clause in each of the following sentences and write it down:

1. The jars on the shelves were packed with sweets of all kinds.
2. The old-fashioned sweets, such as mint humbugs, were kept in special jars.
3. There were bars of chocolate – plain, milk, white, expensive and inexpensive.
4. The chocolate money was wrapped in shiny gold paper.
5. The children, who were only allowed to enter two at a time, pressed their faces against the window pane.
6. Every morning the shop would open without fail at 8 a.m.
7. At Christmas and Easter, high days and holidays, the shop stocked unusual confectionery.

Remember The *main clause* makes sense on its own and is the most important part of the sentence.

The Subordinate Clause

In a longer sentence we often add a **subordinate clause** to the **main clause**. *Subordinate* means *second to something else.*

The subordinate clause does not make sense on its own:

- **main clause**
  The ice rink was popular
  subordinate clause
  when it first opened.

or

- **subordinate clause**
  When it first opened
  main clause
  the ice rink was popular.

A Identify the subordinate clauses in these sentences and write them out:

1. Sophie regularly visited the ice rink, which was open each day.

2. Jack, who could not skate very well, lacked Sophie's skill.

3. He decided to attend so that he could learn how to skate.

4. Before going on to the ice Sophie and Jack put on their boots.

5. Jack, who was very nervous, looked at the crowded rink.

6. Jack watched Sophie who skated confidently.

7. One skater spun round then jumped in the air.

8. Sophie waved to Jack who clung to the edge.

Remember A *subordinate clause* is secondary to a *main clause* and does not make a sentence on its own.

Sentence Building

A Follow the instructions below to build sentences. The first one is done for you.

Copy and Complete	
Start with a **noun**.	The lion
Add a **verb**.	The lion sleeps
Add an **adjective**.	The exhausted lion sleeps
Add an **adverb**.	The exhausted lion sleeps soundly
Add a **phrase** telling where.	The exhausted lion sleeps soundly in the shade of a tree.

1. Start with a noun.
  Add a verb.
  Add an adjective.
  Add an adverb.
  Add a phrase telling where.

2. Start with a noun.
  Add a verb.
  Add a clause telling why.

3. Start with a noun.
  Add an adjective.
  Add another adjective.
  Add a verb.
  Add an adverb.

4. Start with a noun.
  Add a verb.
  Add an adjective.
  Add a phrase telling why.

B Create your own patterns and write sentences based on them.

Remember You can make your sentences grow by adding different parts of speech.

Paragraphs (1)

The opening sentence of a **paragraph** often makes a statement about the topic that will be in the paragraph. This is called a **topic sentence**. The other sentences in the paragraph give more information about what the topic sentence says.

A Write out each of these topic sentences and finish them. Then choose two of them to start paragraphs. Under each one, write three or four sentences to add details and explanations.

1. My school building is _____ .

2. The teachers in my school _____ .

3. We study _____ .

4. I would like to change three things about _____ .

5. The way to get the most out of education is _____ .

B You may wish to complete your report on your school by writing paragraphs on the other topics as well.

Remember The opening sentence of a *paragraph* is called a *topic sentence* because it tells us what the topic will be.

86

Paragraphs (2)

A Imagine you are an alien from another planet. You are visiting Earth to get information. Your assignment is to write an article about Earth children. List what you have discovered about each of these categories. Add two categories of your own.

1. What children do.

2. How children get along with adults.

3. Problems children have.

B Choose three of the five categories. On a separate piece of paper, write one **paragraph** on each of the categories to form your report. Add any illustrations you think might be helpful to the beings on your home planet.

Remember A *paragraph* is a group of sentences about the same idea or topic. Use several paragraphs when you are writing an account or story.

Grammar

A The following notes tell you how to look after a new kitten. Read them carefully.

● Use the notes to write two paragraphs about looking after a new kitten. You should write in sentences.

- Keep your kitten in one room until it is used to its new home.
- Make sure doors and windows are closed and fireplaces guarded.
- Do not let your kitten outside for at least a week.
- If you have a garden take the kitten out for short periods.
- Keep it away from busy roads.
- Make sure it has a warm bed of its own, away from draughts.
- Feed your kitten good quality fresh food which it can digest.
- Feed it small meals, often.
- Teach your kitten to use a litter tray.
- Always keep the litter tray in the same place.
- If the kitten makes a mess, take it to the spot and speak to it firmly.
- Do not shout at your kitten if it makes a mess.
- Brush and comb your kitten regularly.
- Talk to your vet about when your kitten should be vaccinated.